# Changing Woman of the Apache

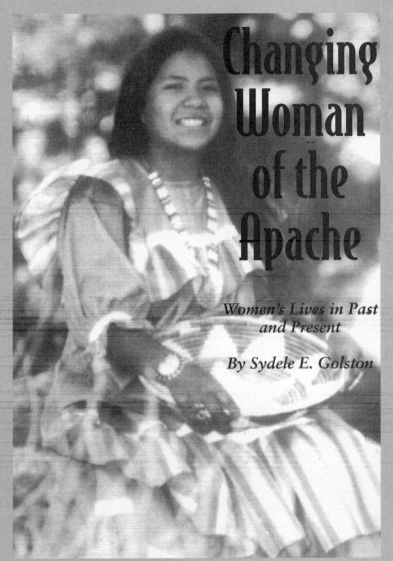

# Changing Woman of the Apache

*Women's Lives in Past and Present*

*By Sydele E. Golston*

*American Indian Experience*
Franklin Watts
*A Division of Grolier Publishing*
New York  London  Hong Kong  Sydney
Danbury, Connecticut

# for
# Maggie
# and
# John

*Title page: Carla Dan Goseyun*

Map by Gary S. Tong
Photographs copyright ©: Goseyun Family: title page,
pp. 24, 35, 36, 42, 44, 47 (both), 49, 52, 53, 55, 58;
Arizona Historical Society: pp. 27 (54008), 65 (41141),
69 (13970), 73 (65248), 84 (13026), 87 (41161), 90
(43392), 94 (25643), 105 (25650), 106 (30411), 107
(48481), 108 (22750), 110 (4575), 114 (50095), 120
(4267), 129 (4577); Lofgreen Photography: p. 33; Syd
Golston: pp. 61, 97, 99, 122; Rick Sanchez: p. 39.

Library of Congress Cataloging-in-Publication Data

Golston, Sydele E.
Changing woman of the Apache: women's lives in past
and present / by Sydele E. Golston.
p.   cm.
Includes bibliographical references and index.
ISBN 0-531-11255-1
1. Changing Women Ceremony (Apache rite)—Juvenile
literature. 2. Apache women—Rites and ceremonies—
Juvenile literature. 3. Apache women—Social life and
customs—Juvenile literature. I Title.
E99.A6G644   1996
305.48'8972—dc20              95-36349   CIP

# Contents

# Preface

*The traditions of the women have, since time immemorial, been centered on continuance, just as those of the men have been centered on transitoriness. . . . He is what comes and goes, she is what continues, what stays. When we shift our attention from the male, the transitory, to the female, the enduring, we realize that the Indians are not doomed to extinction, but rather are fated to endure. What a redemptive, empowering realization that is! As the Cheyenne long have insisted, no people is broken until the heart of its women is on the ground. Then they are broken. Then they will die.*

—*Paula Gunn Allen,* The Sacred Hoop: Recovering the Feminine in American Indian Traditions

Laguna Indian writer Paula Gunn Allen wrote these words at the close of her book, in a chapter she called "Stealing the Thunder." The chapter title lingers ominously in my head. I am not an Indian, and that is the bad news. Although Allen referred to male-dominated culture and interpretation of experience, I fear that I have also stolen the thunder because I am not an Apache woman and yet I presume to tell the story of Apache women, sharing a culture and an experience that are not mine.

I have spent my adult life as a history teacher. I am a Jew, and all four of my grandparents arrived in this country from Russia at the turn of the century. It took me some time to realize that this is the good news here.

My friend Paul Wieser, an Arizona educator who has devoted his career to teaching young people about the Holocaust, is not Jewish; I tell him that he is the great hope. Jews struggle to keep that agenda before the students in our classrooms, but it will survive in the curriculum only if non-Jews care that everyone remembers. I hope that the Apache will be glad that a non-Indian teacher wants students to know not only the male and transitory in their history, the genocide that even textbooks begin to acknowledge, but that she wants them to read about the female and enduring: about Changing Woman and the generations of Apache women who walk with her toward the rising sun.

I also want to share my feelings about history itself, about what is important for students to know. History comprises the aggregate experience of all of us, not just of those who passed laws or made war or had power. Critics of this new, inclusive concept warn us not to spare a moment devoted to Henry Clay so that we can spend it with experiences like those of Apache women. If you must have Apache history, say those critics, it is about Geronimo and Cochise and Victorio. But Paula Gunn Allen would tell you the critics are wrong. Especially they are wrong when it comes to students, that are becoming adults who seek and question . . . or those who don't. I want the widest possible horizon for those students.

In preparing this book, I had help from many sources. I thank first four Apache women, Anna Early Goseyun and her daughters Jeanette, Carla, and Carmen, whom you will meet on these pages. Anna and her girls have been generous with their time, their words, and their warmth. My guides to the interpretation of what I read and saw were Western Apache scholar Crown Dancer, and laughing friend Edgar Perry, who helped me literally word by word. I am glad I found Dave Edgar, teacher at Whiteriver Middle School, with whom I exchanged jobs for a week one April; Dave and Corinna Edgar and their daughters were my hosts during research trips, and kindred spirits always.

I am grateful to the women of Whiteriver who gave me interviews, especially Bonnie Lavender Lewis, Gladys Ethelbah Lavender, and Myrna Guenther Hillyard. I ask all the women I interviewed to forgive the inevitable mistakes I have made in this account.

My colleagues Suzanne Cahill, Stephanie Grant, John Kriekard, Bob Mier, and Ruth Stromer helped to make it possible for me to research and write. I also thank two instrumental educators: Harvard Classics Professor Gregory Nagy, during whose summer NEH seminar this book actually began, and Wesley Benito, Education Director of the White Mountain Apache Tribe, who first invited me to visit Whiteriver to witness a Changing Woman ceremony.

It was a privilege to work with editor Lorna Greenberg at Franklin Watts.

Finally, I thank my children and my parents for their encouragement and their love. The linking of generations is what this story is all about, after all.

*Syd Golston*

# Changing Woman of the Apache

# ≈|≈
# Ndee: The People

They were "Ndee"—"The People." Usin the Creator, the Giver of Life, had placed them on the earth, which was then filled with monsters, in a land of desert valleys and sacred mountains. Their mother was Changing Woman, the first person, who survived a great flood. Usin gave her two sons, Killer of Enemies and Child of the Water, who slayed the monsters and made the land safe for The People. Their homeland was rich with animals to hunt— bear, deer, elk and antelope, rabbits, squirrels, and birds; everywhere there were plants to feed them—agave, pine nuts, and berries. They traveled with the seasons, following the herds and the harvest times for wild foods, living in brush-covered homes that the women built at each campsite. In solemn ceremonials, they thanked Usin and their guardian mountain spirits for the good life that had been given to them.

The People lived in large family groups. Husbands joined the extended families of their wives. Women were the more important providers for the groups; men's hunting only supplemented the foods the women gathered and raised. Females were honored, especially as they entered adolescence, when a four-day festival was held. During this time a young girl became Changing Woman, the mother of The People. The ceremony represented the constant re-creation of the world of the Ndee and the renewal of the entire community.

And then the white strangers came. The People were pursued from their lands, and the animals that fed them dwindled in number. The People raided others to survive, and taught their children to flee and hide out in the mountains they knew so well. Their camps were attacked and their families slaughtered, and they answered murder with murder. They used the land, inhospitable to the Anglos,* to their advantage. Their young men could run at a grueling pace, hardly stopping for days at a time, and could ride for long periods without rations, holding pebbles under their tongues to keep the saliva flowing. A small band could confound an army of thousands. They kept their traditions and their ceremonies faithfully, even in the hardest times. In desperation, they finally agreed to live on the reservations that the Anglos had mapped out for them.

*"Apachu"—"the enemy"—was the Zuni name given to the group of hunter-gatherers and raiders who arrived in today's southwestern United States sometime between A.D. 1100 and 1500. They traveled in the massive Athapaskan migration from west-central Canada, either down the eastern slopes of the Rockies or through the Utah Great Basin region, first to*

---

*Anglos is a term used for all non–Native-American people.

*the plains, where some remained, and then to the highlands and deserts of New Mexico and Arizona. Subgroups of the migration established themselves, while displacing, sometimes violently, the Indians already there: the Kiowa and Lipan Apache in what is now Kansas, the Jicarilla and Mescalero Apache in New Mexico, the Navajo and the Chiricahua and Western Apache in Arizona. The Spaniards, who claimed sovereignty in those lands in the sixteenth century, called the people "Apache" and the portion of New Spain which they inhabited "La Gran Apacheria." They regarded the Apache as enemies, who became even more dangerous opponents when they adopted the horses and guns the Spaniards brought to the Southwest.*

*Mexican independence in 1821 changed the ownership of the Gran Apacheria, but not the relationship between the Apache and the authorities. The Mexican government offered gold for Apache scalps: one hundred pesos for a man's, fifty for a woman's, and twenty-five for a child's. Apache raids were answered by the military destruction of entire camps; Geronimo lost his mother, wife, and three children when the Mexican army burned a camp to the ground and scalped the inhabitants.*

*In 1848, the Apacheria passed finally into the hands of the United States, victorious in the Mexican War. The Apache became the enemy of American settlers and the United States Cavalry. Some groups, notably the Western Apache, accepted treaties and resettlement on reservations established in Arizona and New Mexico, but others refused. Warrior bands roamed under the dread chiefs Cochise, Mangas Coloradas, Victorio, Juh, Nana, and Naiche with the shaman Geronimo. General George Crook enlisted scouts from the Western Apache to help the cavalry to chase them in the 1870s. A tiny Chiricahua band waged the final and fiercest resistance, marked by atrocities on both sides. Geronimo's surrender to General Nelson Miles finally ended the bloody struggle in 1886. Through the entire period, no Indian tribe was considered as savage as the Apache or as much an obstacle to "Manifest Destiny"—the pursuit of Anglo control of all lands from the Atlantic to the Pacific.*

Ndee, the Apache, have two histories, then. It is only in the reservation period, at the end of the nineteenth century, that these two stories join. From that time forward, the record from both inside and outside the tribe is the same, and it is a difficult story with a happier ending.

For over fifty years, until the Indian Reorganization Act of 1934, the United States government tried without success to achieve the assimilation of the Apache, with little regard for their cultural and spiritual traditions. Apache children were taken from their parents to attend schools where they were dressed in Anglo style, taught exclusively in English, and punished for speaking Apache; still, the people kept their language alive by teaching it to their children. They converted to the Christianity of the missionaries who came to the Southwest; most are devout Christians today, but they have maintained their ceremonial traditions as well.

The Apache are beginning to prosper once again, as twentieth-century American farmers, ranchers, and entrepreneurs, and the roots of Apache culture remain alive as one example, the Fort Apache Reservation in east-central Arizona is home to a modern lumber mill, a ski resort, and a lucrative casino; its public schools have computer labs and college board exams. Almost every weekend

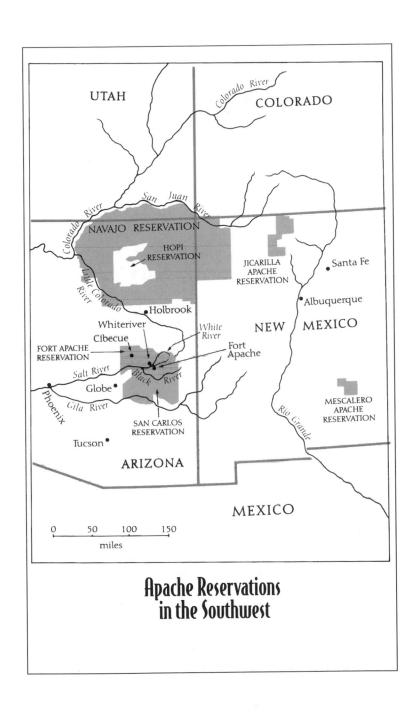

# Apache Reservations in the Southwest

from April through October on the reservation, one or more young girls become Changing Woman in a beautiful and elaborate four-day ceremony called the "Sunrise Dance." The Apache have joined a new world, without losing entirely the traditions of the old one.

*The Apache, it seems to me, have a special gift: the ability to endure. Our beliefs tell us that we were created in the land where we now live during an age when supernatural beings lived as people upon the earth. We were given a religion, language, and traditions to follow.*

*We have since seen much change. Newcomers have arrived in our land. Some have sought to destroy us. Others have desired to re-create us in their own image, to have us give up our language and culture. Our children were sent to boarding schools, and were punished for speaking in their own tongue. Much of our land was taken when it was discovered to be rich in resources.*

*Yet we have survived. Our Apache language and beliefs are respected by the majority. The Apache past is still dramatically verbalized in ceremonial song and taught to apprentice medicine men. Ancient puberty rites are still practiced by our daughters. . . .*

*We hold to our ways so we will know who we are, and to help us feel good about our existence upon the earth. We do not reject the modern technological world. We reach for it to improve the quality of our lives and to create a secure environment where we can safely pursue our Apache ways. . . .*

*We of the White Mountain tribe on the Fort Apache Reservation are but one nation of the Apache. Others of us live on reservations scat-*

*tered throughout Arizona and New Mexico, with
more in Oklahoma. They, like us, desire to live in
harmony with neighbors of all colors. We ask
only to be respected and accepted for what we
are—a people with conviction and our own
unique way of looking at the universe: an Apache
people!*

—Ronnie Lupe, Tribal Chairman,
White Mountain Apache

# ≈2≈ The Legend of Changing Woman

In the beginning, Usin the Giver of Life sent Changing Woman to live all alone upon the earth. No other human creature dwelled there, only giant monsters that roamed the land. Usin warned her of a great flood coming and directed her to find a large abalone shell, in which she was to place food and fresh water and a curved-handle walking cane. Changing Woman, White Painted Woman, crawled into the abalone shell as the flood waters raged and rose, and she floated in her shell on top of the water.

After many days, the waters fell and Changing Woman crawled from her shell onto the sand. Nothing grew on the sand, not even grasses or bushes, and she sat down to wonder what would be and what she should do. Usin spoke to her then, and told her to take her walking stick and climb to the top of the mountains, where the sun's rays first struck.

Changing Woman knelt on the mountaintop and waited. On the first, second, and third days, the clouds failed to part and the sun never shone. On the morning of the fourth day, she sat up on her knees again and she turned her head away. Just then, the sun came up and its beams streamed out and penetrated her body. Changing Woman became pregnant by the sun and gave birth to a boy, called Killer of Enemies.

Changing Woman lived in terror of the monsters roaming the earth, and she feared especially the Owl Man Giant who stalked her, seeking a baby that he could eat. She prayed to Usin, who told her to walk out again, this time into the desert. Usin said, "You must have a child by the rain. That baby, when he is born, you must call Child of the Water. Do not let the Giant seize him, for he will surely kill him. You must hide him under your hearth." Changing Woman lay down on the desert floor, and the storms, thunder, and lightning came, and the rains flowed into her. Four days later, she gave birth to Child of the Water and took him back to her fireside. She dug a deep hole beneath the fire pit and hid the baby there, so that Owl Man Giant would not see him. She loved this baby, and every day she cried and wondered how she was going to save the child from Owl Man Giant.

The child stayed under the fire, and his mother took him from his hiding place only to nurse him. One day she played with him for a few moments after he drank and, as she fondled her little son, he began to make the small cries that a baby makes. She quieted him instantly, for she knew that the time approached when Owl Man Giant would arrive. Quickly, she put Child of the Water back into the hole beneath the hearth.

The moment the baby was again hidden, Owl Man Giant stamped into the clearing carrying his basket and his knife and he said, "I have heard something that is good to eat! I have heard a baby crying. Where is that baby?" Changing Woman told him, "You can see that I am all alone here." Still Owl Man Giant insisted, "I heard a baby crying!"

She said, "I am very, very lonely for a child. Sometimes I sit alone and make for myself the sound of an infant crying." Owl Man Giant was suspicious. "Let me hear you cry like a baby." Changing Woman made the sounds of a baby whimpering, and Owl Man Giant left her, but he did not believe her. She prayed that Child of the Water would hurry and grow big so that he and his brother could slay the monster.

Months passed. One afternoon, Changing Woman took the baby from his hiding place and she sang to him as she cleaned him with a piece of cloth. Child of the Water was growing larger, and after he was washed, she held his little arms and walked him on his toddler legs around the soft ground near her fire. Suddenly she remembered, "Giant will be coming! I must put the baby back again." She hid him, but she forgot about the cloth soiled with the infant's excrement, which lay beside her.

Owl Man Giant strode into the clearing and looked around him. He speared the cloth with his knife and held it up. "There must have been a baby here! There is its green and yellow waste upon this rag!"

Changing Woman replied, "You know that I long for a child. Sometimes I pretend that I have one, and I make a cloth to look like this." Owl Man Giant squinted. "Show me how you do that," he said. Changing Woman thought quickly and cleverly. Large bees swarm on the sotol plant and leave their honey there, which looks green and yellow like a baby's excrement. She had some of this honey, which she smeared on the cloth next to Child of the Water's stain. Owl Man Giant could not tell the difference, and so she got the best of him again.

But the giant spied tiny footprints on the ground at his feet. He said, "Ho ho! Now these are the tracks of a baby! I will have something good to eat." But Changing

Woman responded that she often made little tracks around the fire in her loneliness for a child. With the outside of her clenched hand she made a print in the dust, and added the marks of toes with her fingertips. Again Changing Woman fooled the giant.

At last, Child of the Water grew into boyhood and was old enough to join Killer of Enemies and fight the monsters on the earth. Changing Woman taught her sons all the skills that Apache warriors must know, and she made arrows of grama grass and tipped them with thunder flints of obsidian, and gave the brothers sacred blue turquoise to carry with them. The sons went out and killed Owl Man Giant and the other monsters, so that the world would be safe for The People. They carried pieces of meat back to the camp of their mother, who had been sick with worry over them.

Changing Woman saw the boys returning with the meat, and she gave a long, high cry of delight. This is the sound that the godmothers make at the Sunrise Dance puberty rites for girls, the sound of Changing Woman's victory and her love.

White Painted Woman grew old, but she was always able to recapture her youth. She lives in an endless cycle of childhood, maidenhood, midlife, and old age. When she has become elderly and infirm, she leans upon her curved walking staff and heads toward the east and the rising sun. After a while, she sees her young self approaching from a distance and when the two meet, they join and Changing Woman is reborn. It is this rebirth, given through her to all the Apache, that is celebrated in the ceremony of the Sunrise Dance. She is resiliency and renewal . . . the mother of a people.[1]

*Jeanette Goseyun*

# ≈3≈
# Sunrise Dance: The Gift of Changing Woman

*You have started out on the good earth;*
*You have started out with good moccasins;*
*With moccasin strings of the rainbow, you have*
*started out;*
*With moccasin strings of the sun's rays, you have*
*started out;*
*In the midst of plenty you have started out.*[1]

The Apache celebrate a girl's passage from girlhood to young womanhood in four days of splendor. The ceremony, both solemn and joyous, re-creates the origin of the Ndee on this earth, and it commemorates the sacredness of women and the survival of the tribe. It secures blessings for all, along with the happy future it bestows upon the girl.

# Na'i'es

The ceremony is often referred to now as a Sunrise Dance. Other names are "The Changing Woman Ceremony" and "The Gift of Changing Woman." Its Apache title, "*Na'i'es*,"* means "getting her ready." The ceremony prepares the girl to live a long, useful life as a provider and mother to the next generation. Days of song cycles lead her through all the periods of her life, from youth and young womanhood to adulthood and old age. As the girl actually personifies the holy first woman of the Ndee

> *Reflections of a Sunrise Dance*
> - *a time to share*
> - *a time to give*
> - *a time to sing*
> - *a time to dance*
> - *a time to rejoice*
> - *a time to celebrate life*
> - *a time to renew friendships*
> - *a time to make new friends*
> - *a time to gather with family*
> - *a time to gather with clan relatives and friends*
> - *a time to give thanks*
> - *a time to remember who we are*
> - *a time to set aside our differences*
> - *a time to reaffirm our traditional beliefs*
> - *a time to forgive*
> - *a time to listen*
> - *a time to pray*
> - *a special time for a young woman coming of age*
> - *a special time for my Carla*
>
> —Anna L. Goseyun

* The literal meaning of "Na'i'es" is "massage her with feet."

for a time, she acquires goodness and strength from Changing Woman, which she shares with others through the blessing powers that she holds for the duration of the ceremony.

*Na'i'es* is retained by the Western Apache as the strongest link to traditional life and values. Other ceremonies, briefer and more private, are still occasionally enacted, but the full community celebrates its heritage publicly when a girl comes of age.

Almost all girls became Changing Woman in the old times, but most girls passing into adolescence today have either a short private blessing or none at all. Now only the most traditional families pursue the costly full ceremony. Despite the effort and expense (which can con-

*A Changing Woman ceremony forty years ago, Whiteriver Fairgrounds.*

sume a significant part of a family's income), about twenty *Na'i'es* celebrations take place every year from April to October, on the Fort Apache Reservation. They are always held on weekends, due to the twentieth-century workweek. Some tribal divisions hold group ceremonies; the Mescalero mark the ritual on July Fourth. However, those Western Apache families who hold them still perform the Changing Woman Ceremony for an individual girl. The letter Anna Goseyun enclosed with the invitation to her daughter Jeanette's Sunrise, and the poem "Reflections of a Sunrise Dance," which she wrote for her daughter Carla's dance, show that relatives share the undertaking or it cannot take place.

> *I am extending this invitation to you and your family to participate with me and my family in a coming-of-age ceremony for my youngest daughter, Jeanette Dan Goseyun. It will be a special occasion in her life and my gift to her, to help prepare her for this journey in life. It is a time of spiritual sharing and giving of ourselves in whatever manner that is most meaningful.*
>
> *In the past, I have relied on family members, clan relatives, and friends to support me. Once more I am asking for your assistance in this time in my daughter's life. I know and understand that these times are tough and sometimes it is difficult to provide for our own families.*
>
> *Keeping this in mind, I will appreciate whatever you can do to assist. If you cannot be with me physically, please keep us in your thoughts and prayers during this time.*
>
> *I hope it will be a time of spiritual renewal and a time to remember who we are, as we continue to utilize those spiritual and traditional gifts that were given by Usin to our Apache people.*
>
> —*Anna L. Goseyun*

Carla Goseyun became Changing Woman on a July Saturday in Whiteriver, Arizona. Her younger sister Jeanette followed on a September Saturday, two years later. Carla's and Jeanette's dances varied in some details, since Carla's medicine man was Harris Burnette, who had been trained in the Whiteriver tradition, and Jeanette's was Franklin Stanley, who sang in the San Carlos tradition. Both ceremonies differed somewhat from the older ceremonies recorded by scholars who had studied rites in New Mexico, Whiteriver, and nearby Cibecue. The similarity of the ceremonies over time and place, not the variation, is remarkable. In this account, photographs and descriptions of Jeanette's and Carla's ceremonies are combined with historical material.

The Ndee received the *Na'i'es* tradition from Changing Woman herself. After the people had prospered and multiplied on the earth, made safe for them by her sons, White Painted Woman said:

> *From here on we will have the girl's puberty rite. When the girls first menstruate, you shall have a feast. There shall be songs for these girls. During this feast the masked dancers shall dance in front. After that there shall be round dancing and face-to-face dancing.*[2]

White Painted Woman taught the Ndee how to perform *Na'i'es*; the girl was to dress exactly as Changing Woman had dressed. It was important that the ceremony continue to be enacted just as she wished it.

As soon as a girl who had consented to celebrate *Na'i'es* began her monthly flow, parents began intensive preparations for the ceremony, which would take place the next spring or summer. Planning had certainly begun before this, for families knew generally that the time approached. Relatives and respected family friends, the *Ndee daagoyąąné*, or "wise people," were contacted for their help and advice; the older family members especially were consulted in the choice of the medicine man who would be the girl's Singer and of the woman who would be her godmother and the co-sponsor of her dance.

The responsibilities of the godparents were especially heavy. The godmother agreed to take the role of the *na'i ǩes'ń,* or Attendant to the girl during her dance, and to watch over her as she grew up; the godparents also had to live at their own camp at the dance site, to give a huge dinner for the girl, and to help in all preparations. The relationship between the godparents and the girl was a lasting one, marked by a special form of address that demonstrated mutual obligation. The great honor of serving as Attendant was extended to a wise and generous woman of high esteem from another clan, the kind of woman the family hoped their daughter would become. The woman chosen was strong and vigorous, with a friendly manner and healthy children; the ceremony fostered these attributes for the girl, and much of her instruction came from her godmother.

The selection of the godmother was a mutual agreement. An eagle feather and a prayer stone, a piece of turquoise, were offered to the prospective *na'i ǩ'es'ń,* and she could accept it or refuse it. The girl's family arrived at dawn at the woman's home, bringing gifts. The eagle feather was placed upon the woman's foot, and if she picked it up, she had assented to becoming the girl's godmother. If the feather was refused, it could be offered to other women in turn, up to a total of four. The number four is sacred to the Apache; it represents the four directions of the world—east, west, north, and south—and appears throughout traditional practice.

Anna Goseyun recalled vividly the giving of the feather, *its'os ba'ilzah,* to Carla's and Jeanette's godmothers. Each time it was an adventure to all to climb into the family van, packed with gifts and groceries, before the sun rose on a cold winter morning, on the special errand.

Carla's godparents lived almost an hour from Whiteriver, in Cibecue, where Anna had grown up. "In our eyes, Glenn and Phoebe Cromwell were a couple with good moral standing in the community and strong in their traditional ways. . . . We did this in the winter before Carla's dance, and because the element of surprise is important, we made the request in the early morning hours before sunrise."[3] After his wife accepted the feather, Glenn Cromwell spoke movingly about becoming part of Carla's family from that day on.

Jeanette's godmother, Ruth Massey Key, was a young woman with small children, and had never served as *na'i ǩes'n* before. Anna drove her family and her sister, Judy DeHose, a member of the tribal council, through sleet and snow to reach the Key home on a cold March morning.

"We brought four of everything: bags of flour, tins of baking powder, boxes of fruit, blankets and shawls. We also gave some money. Ruth was so humble when we two older women offered her the feather." Anna was at that time a Juvenile Court Judge, and the young mother was being asked to serve as a role model to Jeanette by two community leaders.

The choosing of a medicine man or Singer to perform the ceremony is equally important, and it is also arranged by the predawn acceptance of an eagle feather and a turquoise prayer stone. In past times, the medicine man might expect to receive horses, saddles, and blankets at the conclusion of *Na'i'es*, but today a payment of several hundred dollars is given at the time he accepts. The medicine man must pay for dancers, drummers, and singers who accompany him in performing the rite. Anna noted that a special closeness was also forged between her girls and the medicine men who sang for them.

Anna's preparations included some modern touches in addition to the traditional ways. A professional photographer took pictures of Carla and Jeanette with some of the articles used in the ceremonial: the eagle feathers, pollen, and burden baskets. The portrait of Jeanette with her godparents, Arden and Ruth Key, shows her holding the feather that symbolized their new role in her life. The photographs were used as backgrounds on the invitations Anna sent to her extended family, her Bamboo Warrior clan (one of sixty-six clans in the White Mountains), and to her friends; Anna, an eloquent writer, composed a poem for Carla's invitation and a letter for Jeanette's. (See pages 26 and 28.)

As the months passed, preparations intensified. A special task was the making of the ceremonial dress, which was prayed over as it was sewn. Five mule-deer skins were tanned and stained yellow, the traditional color worn by Changing Woman. Additional hides were needed to stand upon and to make knee-high beaded moccasins with the characteristic Apache turned-up toes. Hunting parties, acting in kindness, would donate deer to the family of a girl about to become White Painted Woman. An ample supply of deerhide symbolized prosperity for the girl; hunts would always bring days of plenty, and she would never be hungry.

The dress had two parts, an ankle-length skirt and a full poncho top, both heavily fringed and decorated with tiny metal cones that tinkled as the girl danced. The tinklers of the past were made from metal taken in raids on the Mexican towns; later they were cut from tin food cans. Some girls wear the poncho top over a long cotton camp dress, but both Carla and Jeanette had full buckskin outfits, sewn by a friend. They also had special camp dresses made by Mark Kessay, who donated his labor.

A beaded "T" necklace and baskets of the finest work were also made for the girl's special days. They

*Left to right: Jeanette Goseyun, her godfather, Arden Key, and her godmother, Ruth Massey Key.*

were decorated with the spiritual designs of Changing Woman: the sun, the morning star, the crescent moon, and in the colors of the four directions: black for the east, yellow for west, white for north, and blue or green (both the same Apache word, *dotl'izh*) for south. A song in the ceremony referred to the necklace:

*The words of Killer of Enemies, good through*
*long life,*
*Have entered you;*
*They have entered you by means of your*
*necklace;*
*Your necklace has gone into your body,*
*For its power is good.*[4]

Christian symbols were added to Jeanette's necklace, as
Anna explained: "The first medallion shows four arrows
and four feathers—black, white, yellow, and blue, the
colors of the directions. In the center circle you can see
Mother Mary. In the bottom one is a hummingbird. We
think the hummingbird is a happy symbol, and it is
sacred. Has one ever flown right to you? When a hummingbird flies up to you, we believe that it is coming with
a message for you."

Anna pointed to a conical basket fringed in tinklers.
"There is Jeanette's burden basket—it's Apache, but Judy
Chiles made it with a cross on it. She is a White Mountain Apache weaver. Jeanette's pollen basket, the flat one,
is one hundred years old. It's not Apache. It's a Mission
basket with crucifixes on it, that Lee Dixon from the
Puama Reservation in California brought for the ceremony. I meet many people from California at the Catholic
Native American Conferences I attend every summer."

Years ago, the girl's family and the godparents and
the guests could stay in their own wickiups, but today
they must leave their modern houses and work to re-create traditional camps. The family prepared the site for
the ceremony; it had been carefully chosen near a creek,
where the wickiups and the ramadas for cooking and
dining could be set up next to a wide and open dancing
field. After the campsite was ready, it was blessed and
moving in began.

*Jeanette's Sunrise Dance (Saturday morning). Behind her are her godmother, Ruth Key, and Singer Franklin Stanley with assistants. Note the baskets and the three medallions of Jeanette's "T" necklace.*

"It is difficult to choose a camp—because this means sacrificing the luxury of our home for at least two weeks. We become down-to-earth, traditional people. We camp, sleep, and cook outdoors. . . . Tradition dictates that we must build a camp that will shelter up to eight families. The shelter will be built with young green trees from the river bottoms and from along the roadways. It may require ten truckloads—and lots of help." Anna admitted that she was not much of a camper, but Jeanette loved the days in the wickiup. She, Carla, and Anna shared one of the cloth-draped domed structures. She smiled, remembering special evenings of closeness. "It was fun."

During the week preceeding the Sunrise Dance there were nightly celebrations, including enormous festive din-

*Jeanette and Carla follow behind their great-uncle
Steven Lupe, who carries a burden basket as he leads
the group into the camp of Ruth and Arden Key.*

ners given first by the girl's camp and then by the godparents' camp. Each camp walked in procession to the other for the dinner exchanges. Hundreds of people were fed. For Carla's dinner, Anna's mother supervised the preparation of over fifty traditional and modern dishes, acorn and beef stews, roasts, turkeys, and fish, all kinds of vegetables and salads, cakes, pies, and fruits. Two cows had been slaughtered, and mountains of potatoes were peeled and boiled on the outdoor fires. It took an army of women in shifts at the ramadas to do all this.

By Friday, Anna felt, they were approaching the climax. "We are now past the two camp dinners and have already had four nights of singing and special prayers. I had special singers the past four evenings—one was my brother, who is learning the medicine way; another was our tribal chairman, Ronnie Lupe. Mr. Lupe teaches us by his example that it is OK to be a traditional person. I know he is a strong and spiritual person, and it is this tradition that he follows and practices. Friday is a big day. It is now the medicine man's duty to take over."

The medicine man began his work in the early morning hours on Friday. He and his helpers and the godfather purified themselves first in a ritual Apache sweat bath, where water was poured over hot stones and the men sang several of the four-song sets from *Na'i'es* in steaming dimness. When they emerged, they plunged into the cold creek water. Other male guests then used the sweat lodges throughout the morning.

The medicine man and the helpers now made ritual articles. Each of the items had to be crafted slowly and perfectly. If the items were less than perfect, their prayer power might be lost and the ceremony spoiled. Every object contained elements of good fortune for the young woman and her people.

Most important was the decorated wooden cane. It symbolized long life, the greatest gift the ceremony would bring to the girl. She would dance with it throughout the ceremony, and when she was an old woman she could lean upon it. It was carved from a peeled branch of an acorn-bearing oak, painted with yellow ocher, and hung with eagle feathers to protect the girl from illness and with oriole feathers to give her a happy disposition. A bead of turquoise was added for a prayer stone, and long ribbons of black, green, yellow, and white for the four directions were attached. Bells at the end of the crook would jingle with every step of the dance.[5]

Each part of her cane assured the girl a successful Apache womanhood. The wood was cut from a fertile tree that fed the people; she would bear children and feed her family. The oriole is a happy bird that minds its own business and behaves well; the girl would be a cheerful person, never a quarrelsome meddler in the affairs of her neighbors. A medicine man said that wherever she went the four colors of her cane's ribbons would follow, which means that "there would be somebody to watch her, somebody hears her, somebody watches over her and guards her."[6]

The medicine man cut a bamboo reed for a drinking tube and sharpened a wooden twig to make a scratching stick for the girl to use for the next four days. These were bound on a necklace of hide that she would wear around her neck. Drinking with her lips during the rites might bring rain, or cause her to grow whiskers on her chin like a man; scratching with her fingernails would scar her skin.

The medicine man blessed the girl's buckskin dress, a small abalone shell pendant for her forehead, the cane, the drinking tube, and the scratching stick. Three eagle feathers were also sanctified for her. There was a large eagle feather for her hair, which would guide her at *Na'i'es* and hover over her always, even after it was physically removed at the conclusion of the ceremony. A pair

*A ritual wooden cane.*

of smaller eagle feathers, one for each of her shoulders, were also blessed; they would carry her body lightly and easily through her strenuous dancing. The girl, accompanied by women from her camp, arrived at noon carrying breads she had made, and many other dishes for the midday meal for the Singer and his helpers. She was given the ritual items to take back to her wickiup.

Traditionally, the godmother then would bathe the girl and wash her hair in suds from yucca-root soap. This must have made a wonderful cleanser, for the hair of Apache women in the photographs of a century ago was smooth and lustrous. Jeanette Goseyun admitted that she had never tried yucca-root soap. "I had just regular shampoo." The girl would not bathe or wash her hair again for several days.

&

Just before sundown on Friday the celebrants gathered in a clearing for *bi kehilze'*, the dressing of the girl. There the medicine man had carefully placed the ritual items she would wear for the next four days on a blanket, along with drums and a basket of pollen, a sacred substance that represents life to the Apache, in its renewal of growing things. Pollen is a constant element of *Na'i'es*.

The godmother stood with the girl on the blanket before the medicine man Singer, who began the rites by addressing the girl and the people together. He spoke of the ways of the ancestors and the need to follow in good paths—paths that would again be made clear to them during the days of the ceremony. He explained to the girl the events that would follow, and the need for the womanly qualities of endurance, patience, and goodness that her godmother would share with her. He asked her to open her heart to the teaching and the sacred experiences that lay before her.

The Singer directed the steps of the dressing. The godmother tied on the abalone pendant of White Shell Woman so that the small, shining oval lay in the center of the girl's forehead. She fastened eagle feathers to her shoulders, and draped the necklace thong holding her drinking tube and scratching stick around the girl's neck. Finally, the *na'i ʒes'ń* tied the large special eagle plume to the back of her hair, and handed her the cane.

At that moment in Carla Goseyun's ceremony, something happened that electrified the company. Anna recalled it: "I had learned a long time ago that our Creator communicates with us in different ways, although sometimes we are not aware of the signs he gives us. Soon after her godmother put the feather on Carla's head, the feather stood straight up on its own, and it seemed to dance on her head. It was a moving sight. We were told that truly we had an innocent daughter. For me, this incident was a powerful sign."

The girl's innocence is vital to *Na'i'es* :

> *An important part of the ritual was where she blessed each person in the gathering with pollen, and if she assumed the power of White Painted woman fraudulently she could bring very bad luck to those she affected. A girl who was known to have "gone around" with boys might be denied the ceremony; if she undertook the ceremony and was later learned to have had sexual experience, she might even be banished.*[7]

As the dressing procedures were completed, the godmother walked in a circle around the girl, and the Singer began the first of the many four-song cycles of *Na'i'es*. The sets of four songs, and their multiples of twelve, sixteen, or thirty-two, became like a pulse or an internal clock for the girl over the course of the following days. Sometimes, Anna said, girls kept track of the songs on the fringes of their dresses. Pollen from the basket was sprinkled over the girl during the last of the four songs, and the dressing rite was over.

41

*Godmother Phoebe Cromwell fastens an eagle feather
to Carla Goseyun's hair.*

On Friday evening, songs and dancing lasted from sunset to midnight, an early conclusion: this was a "half-night dance," *bidiꞩtii* or the "night before dance." The only illumination on the open field was an enormous bonfire, with crackling sparks that flew skyward. Her partner or Substitute, a slightly older girl (usually a sister or cousin who had already become Changing Woman), stepped in place at the side of the girl, who lifted and planted her cane at each step. The two girls would dance side by side this way frequently during the long rites of the next two days. The supportive relationship they shared at *Na'i'es* made a special and lasting bond between them; Carla Goseyun's partner was her older sister Carmen, and Jeanette's was Carla. The sisters grew very close during their ceremonies.

The girl was ready before dawn on Saturday morning. It was time to prepare for the Sunrise Dance itself, which must start as the first rays of the sun come up from the mountains and strike the abalone shell on the girl's forehead. She laid a deerskin facing eastward over a pile of eight blankets on the ground; four came from the godmother's camp and four from her own. The Singer's helpers covered additional blankets stretching from the deerskin toward the east with an abalone shell that held pollen, a burden basket filled with candy and coins, and many baskets and boxes of fruits and candy. In recent times, some of the boxes hold cans of soft drinks too. This bounty of food and blankets represent Changing Woman's gift of plenty to the girl and to the people.

The girl and her Substitute took their places with reverent concentration at the end of the line of blankets, facing eastward. The Singer and his helpers, five or more men who thumped handheld drums and sang with him, stood behind the girls as they awaited the moment to begin. All these men, including the Singer, wore western-style shirts and wide-brimmed cowboy hats. The guests circled the perimeter of the dance field, just a few at this early hour but more and more throughout the morning; women came in fine camp dresses, with colorful and beribboned full skirts and overblouses, and there were many children.

Jeanette was aware of Singer Franklin Stanley just behind her; he told her at each juncture what was to happen, what she must do, and he explained what would be said in the songs and prayers, in English: "Keep your eyes east now" or "Here you will lie down." She recalled her mother's instruction, to be peaceful and prayerful throughout her dancing. She spoke her own prayers inside her head, prayers especially for the family and friends whom she loved.

*Jeanette and her Substitute, her sister Carla; Singer Franklin Stanley is directly behind them.*

The sun appeared at the crest of the mountains, and a shaft of light struck the shell on the girl's forehead. Six hours of dancing began, to the songs of *Na'i'es*, the *Gozhoo sih* or "full-of-great-happiness" songs.

The girl and her Substitute stepped in place, up and down, up and down. With each step, the jingling cane was lifted and planted, and the tinklers on the ceremonial dress rang lightly. This was a feat of endurance as the day continued and the hot sun rose higher in the sky. The Singer watched the girl carefully to pace the dance, so that she would not become exhausted; at pauses in the song cycles, her godmother lifted the shining hair that streamed down her back, wiped her neck and face with a long handkerchief pinned to the godmother's camp dress of the four direction colors, and gave her water to drink through her drinking tube.

The first songs were about the Creation. When Changing Woman or her sons were named, the godmother "gave the cry," the high-pitched ululation that represented Changing Woman's glad greeting to her sons; one of the alternative names for the godmother is "she who gives the cry." Now and again, older women at the dance also gave the cry. In these early songs, Changing Woman's power was entering the body of the adolescent girl. In the girl's serene face and graceful steps, White Painted Woman reappeared to the people. Visibly, the girl came of age.

Now the *na'i ᶄ'es'ń* became the young woman's partner. She took the girl's cane, planted it in the ground, and helped her to kneel on the deerskin with her arms upraised, in the posture of Changing Woman when the sun's rays entered her body on the mountaintop. As the singing continued, the godmother guided the kneeling girl to sway from side to side, with her face uplifted to the sun.

The next phase of the Sunrise Dance was the massage. Carefully the godmother straightened the girl's body face down, arms at her sides, on the deerskin-covered blankets. As the godmother circled four times in each of four molding songs, she used both her hands and her feet to pull and smooth the girl's entire body and finally her head and face. This massage would give the girl a vigorous and erect body to meet the demands of womanhood; the way the girl received the massage determined whether she would be stooped or straight, weak or strong. The godmother drew the girl to her feet, and many have noticed that the girl seemed physically changed: "she was taller now and more beautiful . . . radiant, in fact, and fully aware that the power was working in her."[8]

Jeanette later said that her legs were hurting her at this point from four hours of dancing, but after Ruth Key's massage, the pain went away. Even a girl as athletic as Jeanette had fears that she would not be strong enough to dance well for such a long time. Girls sometimes built up their endurance for *Na'i'es* in running regimens; Edgar Perry, then director of the White Mountain Apache Cultural Center, ran early every morning with his niece Brenda in the spring before her ceremony.

Midmorning approached, and the ceremony quickened. During the next phase, the godmother planted the girl's cane in the ground four times, each time farther to the east. She pushed the girl forward by her shoulders, and the girl ran up to and around her cane each time. This symbolized living through the phases of her life. As she ran, she "captured" each stage, ensuring longevity. The Singer chanted of the seasons of childhood, young womanhood, adulthood, and old age.

Now the cane was planted in each of the four directions, and again the godmother pushed the girl. She ran around it, followed by many children from the circle of celebrants. In the running to the four directions, Changing Woman gave the girl the lifelong ability to run quick-

*Kneeling as Changing Woman did when impregnated by the Sun*

*The massage*

ly without fatigue. Girls run this portion especially swiftly, with that gift of strength.

Next came the excitement of *shanadi̱k* ("candy, it is
poured"). The Singer dusted the girl with pollen, and
poured a small burden basket of candy, corn kernels, and
coins over her head.

> *After he pours it over her head, everything in all*
> *the baskets gets holy. Not just the stuff from the*
> *basket he pours over her. All the baskets, even the*
> *big ones near the buckskin. Because it is holy, all*
> *those things, everybody wants it. If you get a*
> *piece of candy, you will have plenty food all the*
> *time. If you take one of those corns home and*
> *plant it, you have plenty corn to bring in later on.*
> *You get some money, that means you get rich and*
> *never be poor. The girl's power makes all those*
> *things holy and good to have.*[9]

The children surged forward in glee, and took the fruits
and candy and drinks from the baskets and boxes.

As White Painted Woman, the girl was then blessed
and gave blessings with pollen to a long line of celebrants
who assembled at the end of the Saturday-morning ceremony. Mothers held up infants so she could run her
hands over their limbs to strengthen them, and she used
her pollen-coated fingers with a sure and graceful touch.
Sometimes, the girl held up a baby to the four directions.
An older woman offered an arthritic arm for her to touch
and heal. Her face was solemn, and she showed none of
the fatigue that surely she felt after more than six hours
of ceremonial dancing. At these moments all were aware
of a powerful presence within the girl—a woman's presence in the body of a young teenager.

Carla Goseyun placed her hands about the head of a
toddler boy. Behind her, medicine man Harris Burnette

observed carefully. Following the White Mountain ceremonial style, Burnette had traced a cross of the four directions with pollen on each of Carla's hands. She held infants up to each direction, while blowing her breath to east, west, north, and south. Older accounts indicate that girls would blow or spit into the babies' mouths. Jeanette, in her San Carlos–style ceremony, did not bless and heal celebrants in a blessing line, but she did use her healing powers during her dance. Jeanette massaged her grandmother's leg in her wickiup; Anna recalled that the granddaughter's touch did indeed bring relief. Stories of a girl's power to make babies healthy abound:

> *When my son was a baby, he was only crawling about by the time he should have been walking. A girl was having a puberty ceremony then, so I took my baby to her. She led the baby, making it*

*Carla blesses a baby, as medicine man Harris Burnette looks on.*

*walk to the four directions: east, south, west, and north, just a few steps. Then I told her, "Let him walk today. Tell the Sun to let this baby walk today," so the girl said, "Let this baby walk today." It was summertime, and the corn was getting ripe. I took my baby home, untied him from his carrier, and left him to sit on the ground. Then I went after some roasting ears in the field. When I came back, I saw him standing up, holding to his carrier. In a little while he started to walk to me. When he reached me, he put his arms about my neck. He has never been sick since that time, because he obtained luck from that pubescent girl.*[10]

Often more than a hundred people waited in line for blessings at a ceremony. Changing Woman's power to renew and strengthen the tribe was at its most vivid then. During the dark days of the Apache Wars of the 1870s, after the death of Chief Victorio, a ceremony was held for his granddaughter Beshad'è. Dilth Cleyhen, mother of the girl, mourned her father for the proper period, but wanted a puberty rite to be held, to restore the Apache in those troubled times. The power of Changing Woman is great:

*Apaches believe that whatever wish is made while blessing the girl is certain to come true. . . . A few of these are recorded below.*
*. . . to have a good crop of corn and beans.*
*. . . to make my sick wife get better.*
*. . . my cattle, to get fat for sale time.*
*. . . to cure up my daughter's face.*
*. . . rain.*
*. . . my son in Dallas learning to be a barber, not get into any trouble."*[11]

The Saturday morning celebration concluded with the throwing of the blankets and the deerskin. The girl shook them out and threw them to each direction; symbolically, she would always have a clean wickiup and an abundant camp. When she finished, she was anxious to return to her temporary wickiup to rest.

As the girl slept, the Dwelling Place of Changing Woman, a four-poled tipi, was constructed for her on the dance ground. Four kinds of saplings were used for the tipi, painted in the direction colors with the designs of White Painted Woman. A rope was strung between two of the poles, and eagle feathers were hung on it. Once again, the men's work was meticulous; none of the saplings could be damaged, or another would have to be located. Wood for this night's bonfire, which had to last through sunrise, was piled on the field to the east.

Jeanette, who was ill with the flu during her *Na'i'es*, was awakened gently in the late afternoon on Saturday for family photographs. Remarkably, she looked refreshed and lovely as she stood with her ceremonial articles. That night she was to dance with four other girls as they paired with the Gaan Crown Dancers; it was the most expressive and energetic of the dancing requirements, not performed in place but in swirling circles and patterns. A dance professor who studied *Na'i'es* every summer commented that Jeanette Goseyun, after an exhausting morning and despite her illness, was one of best and most graceful dancers of these steps that she had ever observed.

Everyone looked forward to seeing the Crown Dancers. Anna explained the procedures for Carla's Crown Dancers. "Back in June, we had taken a weekend to have all the special crowns made for this evening's event. Because it is important to do this away from the community, the crowns were made in a secluded area with the medicine man present. Special designs and colors were chosen, and my father, brother, and son were involved.

"Now the time has come for the evening of the Crown Dancers, and everyone waits to see what special designs and colors were chosen for Carla. I had a dress made to match her Crown Dancers' colors—it is beautiful. On this evening, the Crown Dancers will dance to their own special songs, and they will be blessed by four chosen medicine people. It is an honor to do this because

*Jeanette, second from left, poses with her mother and sisters before the evening of the Crown Dancers. Left to right: older sister Carmen, holding the pollen-painting basket, Jeanette, with cane and burden basket, Carla, and Anna Goseyun.*

the Crown Dancers will have special protective powers and blessings this night. My brother, one of the dancers, is the clown. He is the revered dancer because we believe he is the leader and directs what has to be done. . . . They are powerful spiritual beings coming to do what we ask of them—to bless my Carla."

*&*

The sun went down and the crowd assembled for the lighting of the bonfire. The Singer and his assistants

*The evening of the Crown Dancers:*
*Carla and the Gaan are wearing crowns*
*painted expressly for her ceremony.*

began the drumming and singing. The girl was accompanied by four attendants, two chosen by her family and two by her godparents. Jeanette danced with two nieces of Arden and Ruth Key, her friend Anne Dillon, and her sister Carla. The other three girls were also arrayed in buckskin moccasins and fringed dresses, with their finest jewelry. This was traditionally a night for Apache courting, and they were a glorious group.

The audience began to look around in excitement for the entrance of the Gaan, the mountain-spirit dancers. Suddenly, they appeared on the dance ground in the firelight:

> *There they were, five of them in all, walking in single file with the clown last. They cast long, frightening shadows, and they were awesome in appearance, wearing their knee-high buckskin moccasins and fantastic three-or-more-feet-high wooden crowns. They carried painted wands in each hand, their faces were hidden by black masks, and spruce branches were inserted under their belts at the back and sides. Their bodies were painted with bold symbolic designs; the body paint was gray over which black spots and other designs were neatly applied. The clown had black stripes around his legs at four-inch intervals. The awed crowd backed away. . . .[12]*

The Clown carried a "bull-roarer," a wooden wedge on a length of cord, which produced the shrieking sound of the wind in the mountains when whirled. These were moments of magic.

The Gaan danced alone first, thrusting their wands into the ground as they moved, and then they danced with the five young women. Sometimes the Clown came close to the crowd and danced just steps away. Men threw logs onto the fire, sparks flew, and the sky seemed very black and the stars very bright.

*Jeanette, the girls, and the Gaan dance together
near the fire.*

A procession took the guests who wanted to partici-
pate up to and around the Dwelling Place. The girl was
led into the open tipi by the Singer:

> *Killer of Enemies, source of long life,*
> *White Painted Woman has come inside;*
> *She grows up by means of it.*
>
> *The spruce home of White Painted Woman is
> built of long life,*
> *By means of a home built of this she has gone
> inside,*
> *By means of her power of goodness*
> *White Painted Woman has come to her,*
> *By means of it the words have gone inside.*[13]

After the ceremonial dancing, the all-night social dancing commenced, where women and men paired off and lasting relationships might be forged (see Chapter 5). Jeanette retired to her wickiup, where her friend Anne stayed for the night. They talked animatedly before falling into needed sleep:

> White Painted Woman's power emerges,
> Her power for sleep.
> White Painted Woman carries this girl;
> She carries her through long life,
> She carries her to good fortune,
> She carries her to old age,
> She bears her to peaceful sleep.[14]

At first light, the logs still smoldered in an ashen pile on the field. Sunday morning was the last public ceremony, when the Gaan would reappear and the girl would be "painted" with liquid pollen mixed with clay and some corn the girl herself had ground. The girl and her Substitute again took places side by side to begin the dancing; now they stood beneath the poles of the open four-sided Dwelling Place. It was almost over, and the Substitute encouraged the girl for this final effort. The medicine man sang thirty-two more songs before the tipi, which Anna described as the "altar" for the Sunday rites.

The girl's father and godfather had important roles on Sunday morning; they accompanied her in processions through the Dwelling Place. Her father held her cane as she knelt and swayed again on the blankets. At the end, the godfather would paint the crowd from the basket containing clay and pollen liquid.

From the east the Gaan reappeared, startling even in the daylight, dancing forcefully before the girl, their bells shaking as they held their wands above her. They circled around and through the tipi for several song cycles. The painting began when the Gaan leader seized a grass-bundle brush that lay in the flat painting basket and began to coat the girl from head to foot in the deep yellow pollen mixture. Each Crown Dancer and the godfather painted her in turn. The girl's hair and her buckskin dress were quickly clotted; even her face was covered, and she closed her eyes. The *na'i ḵ'es'ñ* wiped away the liquid on her eyelids with her dangling handkerchief.

Her godfather danced beside the painted girl at the head of a line of celebrants. In the photograph, Jeanette held the pollen basket as Arden Key prepared to dip in the brush and brandish it above the crowd, spraying yellow drops over everyone's hair and clothes. It brought good fortune to bear away from *Na'i'es* the stains of pollen drops, and the grass-bundle brush cast them widely, striking celebrants many yards away. The crowd grew louder and more enthusiastic as the last four songs began. They knew that the ceremony was complete, the girl had won her destiny, and their hearts were full of gladness for her. "It's about through with her; it's close to the end. Everybody is yelling, you know. Like a victory, almost literally a victory. They know what she has."[15]

Jeanette said that by this time she was truly thrilled. "I did not want it to end!" She paid no attention to the pollen clay in her eyes and all over her. In fact, she has kept the pollen on her ceremonial dress ever since, although Carla and other girls cleaned and brushed it off.

The perimeter circle broke into happy congratulatory groups. The tipi poles were quickly lowered to the ground. It was over.

There were more moments of delight on Sunday. After the ceremony came gift-giving time; presents were both bestowed and received by the young woman. As family members left to return to homes in other communities, they were given food, blankets, dishes, and other gifts; the family shared the bounty of Changing Woman

*Sunday morning painting, left to right: Ruth Key (beneath tipi), the Crown Dancer, Jeanette, Arden Key, and the godfather*

through these presents and thanked their guests for participating in this sacred time in their daughter's life.

The girl received both great and small gifts. Godmother Ruth Key gave Jeanette a white bicycle, and Arden Key presented her with a tennis racket. Anna's presents included Jeanette's burden basket and the exquisite Navajo bracelet and ring of moonstones and turquoise that she wore during the ceremony; others gave her earrings, beaded necklaces, and jewelry. There were blankets, a traditional gift; and notebooks, a more modern one.

Jeanette's grandmother Ida Early, Anna's mother, performed the final procedure of *Na'i'es* on Monday morning. She removed the ceremonial items that Jeanette wore and placed them properly on a blanket. After this "undressing," Jeanette could finally bathe and wash her hair.

Later Jeanette spoke about becoming Changing Woman. "Ever since I was a little girl, I wanted to do it. It was very special to me, and I still think about it."

*In the east,*
*The White Painted Woman, when she is walking*
*in accordance with the pollen of the dawn,*
*The White Painted Woman is happy over it,*
*She is thankful for it.*
*In the south,*
*She is walking in accordance with the sun's*
*tassels;*
*Long life!*
*From this, there is good,*
*In the west,*
*When the pollen of the abalone shell moves*
*with her, there is good;*
*Long life!*
*If she lives in accordance with it, there is good.*
*In the north,*
*She is the sister of the White Painted Woman;*
*When she is walking in accordance with this,*
*there is good.*
*She is looking at her,*
*She is happy over it,*
*She is thankful for it.*[16]

# ≈4≈
# Childhood

Lieutenant Jack Summerhayes and his wife, Martha, were posted in 1874 to Fort Apache, where they had a baby. Nantucket-bred Martha delighted in the gift of a cradle-board:

> *The seventh day after the birth of the baby, a delegation of several squaws, wives of chiefs, came to pay me a formal visit. They brought me some finely woven baskets, and a beautiful papoose-basket or cradle, such as they carry their own babies in. This was made of the lightest wood, and covered with the finest skin of fawn, tanned with birch bark by their own hands, and embroidered in blue beads; it was their best work. I admired it, and tried to express to them my thanks. These squaws . . . looked about the room, until they found a small pillow, which they laid into the basket-cradle, then put my baby in, drew the flaps together, and laced him into it; then stood it up, and laid it*

*Carmen Goseyun, with infant*
*Dominick in a cradleboard*

*down, and laughed again in their gentle manner,*
*and finally soothed him to sleep. I was quite*
*touched by the friendliness of it all. They laid the*
*cradle on the table and departed.* [1]

Martha Summerhayes was one of the first Anglos to
appreciate the traditional Apache cradleboard, a beautiful and comfortable version of the infant seat that mod-

ern mothers all over the world use today. In the photograph, Carmen Goseyun with infant Dominick shows how a baby in a cradleboard could safely be carried along for days of food gathering on foot and hard travel on horseback across the mountains and canyons of the Southwest.

## Childhood: The Old Times

The Apache baby girl or boy (both called *me'* until about the age of two) spends its first half-year of life in the *ts'aak̲* , or cradleboard. A baby might have two of these, a temporary one hastily made at delivery time and a permanent carrier readied in the days after birth. Often the permanent carrier was made by a female relative, the baby's maternal grandmother or great-aunt or great-grandmother. If a woman had lost babies in the past, she might go to a woman who had successfully raised many children and ask her to make the cradleboard; there were also artisans well known for the beauty of their carriers. If the new baby was born to a family with other healthy children, it was cradled in the board the mother had used with good fortune earlier.

The carrier was both sturdy and cozy for the infant. The cradle maker bent gambel oak into an oval frame, filled it with slats of sotol stalk, and fashioned a hood of narrow peeled arcs of cat's-claw. She attached a strong tumpline, to stretch across the mother's chest or drape across her forehead, so that the mother could carry the board on her back with her hands free to work. She lined the inside with a thick layer of grass and shredded bark, covered by a mattress of softest fawn's hair, also used for the coverlet that tucked in the baby.

The decorations for the cradleboard augured health and contentment for the infant. The baby's father searched for the nest of a verdin, a bird that quickly falls asleep, to obtain verdin feathers for the baby's pillow. The hood held dangles to fascinate the baby and safeguard the baby's health. They were made of squirrels' tails and small stripped pine cones; the squirrel was a good tree climber, so the baby would not fall from pine trees. A small piece of the cactus used for sprains and broken bones warded these off. A bear claw kept sickness away, because of Bear's great power. Glass beads, metal jingles, and stone arrow points enhanced this swaying array for the baby's eyes to follow.

The infant's own umbilicus, wrapped in a scrap of buckskin or cloth, hung from the hood; the Western Apache buried it later in a deer track to ensure hunting prowess for a boy, or in a mescal plant or a cornfield for a girl, so that she would grow up to be a good food provider. There was no formal ceremony for this; the parents might say aloud, "She will prepare quantities of mescal." The umbilicus of Chiricahua daughters was placed in a tree that bore fruit, with the prayer "May she live and grow to see you bear fruit many times."

Close relatives held a short birth ceremony as they placed the newborn into the cradleboard. After pollen was scattered to all four directions, they held the baby up to east, south, west, and north. They chanted a cradlesong prayer, which was repeated when a girl celebrated her Sunrise Dance years later. Sometimes the infant was then named, if some physical feature or event of the birth suggested a name.

Daughters were as welcome as sons, if not more so. The Ndee were a *matrilocal* society, meaning that a husband came to live with the wife's extended family. A daughter would live forever with the parents, and she and her future family would support them in their old age; a son would leave them someday for his wife's camp.

Apache babies cried very little; lives depended on their being quiet if the group was ambushed and had to flee into hiding. Dilth Cleyhen, the infant daughter of Chief Victorio, had such an experience:

*The cradled Dilth-Cleyhen had been slung across her mother's lap. When fairly sure they were unseen, her mother adjusted the ts'aak so that it hung down the side of the horse, secured by means of the tumpline. Then, once again, off they flew. The cradle bumped, jostled, and swayed.*

*Finally, mother, child, and mount slowed, wending their solitary way silently through underbrush.*

*"You were good, my child. You did not cry out. That is how you must always be."*[2]

It was a good sign if an infant did not scream even at birth; such a child would grow up strong, it was said. An infant who fussed in the cradleboard was propped at a new angle or rocked for a moment. The mother took the baby from the carrier to change the soft bark and grass diaper or to feed the child, although sometimes the baby was fed while in the cradleboard. The cradled baby became part of the mother's round of life, taken along to gather foods and on all other errands, hung near the mother on a low bough when not on the mother's back. The close security of the carrier and the fascination of changing scenery helped to lull the child.

Crawling infants were placed in the cradleboard only for traveling somewhere. A walking baby was transported in a shawl sling on the mother's hip or back. Women saved outgrown carriers to use again, if the baby had thrived, but a cradleboard was abandoned in a tree if the baby was sickly or died. A woman who had completed

*An old photograph shows infants in carriers were taken along on food-gathering errands, and propped against a tree.*

her childbearing years hung her cradleboard from a branch and said to it, "You have raised my children safely, so look after them from now on."

A ceremony called "Putting on Moccasins" was held to celebrate the first steps a little boy or girl took, for which small moccasins and either a tiny buckskin dress or shirt were prepared. The shaman called a little girl "Changing Woman" and a little boy "Child of the Water," and on white buckskin he marked tiny footprints with a fist coated in pollen, as Changing Woman had done to fool Owl Man Giant in the creation story. The girl baby was walked in the four directions and blessed with pollen on her head and brow, as she would be marked again in her Sunrise Dance years later. Another brief ceremony took place for the baby's first haircut; the shorn locks were sewn into the child's clothing. The ears of little children of both sexes were pierced because it was believed that the baby would hear things sooner and obey more quickly.

Parents disciplined little ones gently, and they were not weaned for two or sometimes even three years. The Ndee used ingenious methods to stop the occasional crying of toddlers: drops of water were spilled over their foreheads, or a covering placed over their heads until they learned not to whimper. Naughty children were warned that *Goge'* the whippoorwill or Big Owl could punish them:

> *A small child crying from a fit of temper may be stopped by threats of Big Owl, a mythological giant owl who used to carry off children in his great burden basket. "If you don't behave, Big Owl will hear you. He lives near here and he will come and carry you off. You had better stop crying."*[3]

The Gray One, or Clown, of the Gaan mountain-spirit dancers was used to threaten misbehaving children. Sometimes an old man from the camp, wearing a stern expression, might come into the wickiup and the parents would feign turning over children to him if they had acted badly. As children grew older, they learned proper behavior from the legends of the Coyote, the Bobcat, and the other animals, recited to them over winter fires in the wickiup by their parents and grandparents. The stories showed the importance of obedience, hard work, truthfulness, and generosity, and the downfall of those like wayward Coyote, *Ma'ii* in Apache, who lacked such qualities. Here was a lesson about laziness, provided by a story of how Coyote planted corn:

> *Coyote would have to do lots of work if he wanted to raise his corn, but he did not want to do this. "These people here plant their corn, and after it is grown they have to cook it. Me . . . I will cook my corn first and then plant it so when it is grown I won't have to bother about cooking it." . . . Coyote cooked his corn, ate some, and planted the rest. . . . [But] the place that Coyote planted had nothing growing on it at all. Coyote got angry. "You people must have taken the hearts out of the corn seeds you gave to me." "No, we didn't do that, but you cooked the heart out of your corn seeds before you planted. You ought not to have done that."*
>
> —"Coyote Plants Cooked Corn" [4]

Years passed. A little girl was now called `it' é• d´n (girl) until puberty. Although the chances of survival increased greatly for children who weathered the most dangerous first years, the world was still a perilous place. When baby teeth fell out, a child was told to wrap them in grama grass and throw them away in a remote spot, where a witch could never find them. Deaths of someone in the camp would occur, and the children learned that it would bring bad fortune to say their names or to use anything that belonged to them, for fear of summoning the ghost of the deceased. Children wore amulets to counter disease, snakes, bears, witches, and ghosts.

Boys and girls shared many pastimes. They played running games, and sought honey and berries to eat. Girls, as well as boys, learned to use small slings, lances, and bows and arrows; to hunt rabbits; and to saddle and ride horses. Older children of both sexes were encouraged to toughen themselves by running and swimming rigorously, even on cold mornings when ice had formed on the water.

The play of children also showed some gender differences. Much of little girls' play emulated their mothers' tasks and tools. The writer Grenville Goodwin described games played by Western Apache girls. They treasured miniature cradleboards fashioned for them by adults, in which they placed dolls or occasionally pets. One seven-year-old delighted her family by bringing inside her toy baby-carrier, draped with a silk handkerchief. She drew the kerchief back for her mother and grandparents, to reveal her small black puppy laced inside, fast asleep. Girls used doll-sized clay pots and burden baskets, and enjoyed elaborate play in model wickiups:

*Inez, Katherine, and Dora were playing together. Each one built herself a small wickiup, just big enough to get into. The frames were made of old sticks and covered with a blanket. This is typical of play wickiups, and no child was seen trying to cover a wickiup with grass and other brush, as is*

*Four young girls with bows and arrows, in a photograph from an earlier period. Apache girls learned many outdoor skills.*

*done in building real dwellings. Inside two of the play dwellings the little girls lit tiny fires made from chips they had picked up about the yard. Within the third a little girl was pretending to grind meal on a metate. This was a flat stone on which she was grinding dirt. They were in and out of their play camps for almost an hour or more, carrying their dolls about, putting them down, or taking them inside.[5]*

Intentionally, Apache dolls did not look very lifelike. They might suggest a corpse if they did. The Apache never liked the dolls with which Anglo children played, because they resembled real babies too closely.

Children of the Ndee learned prayer and ritual by observing their importance in everyday existence, long before particular prayers and the spiritual legends were taught to them. Little girls might stage an imitation of the Changing Woman ceremony, with makeshift cane, scratching stick, and massage. Boys sometimes made toy bull-roarers like those used by the Gaan, wooden wedges attached to strings, which made a shrieking noise when whirled through the air.

Women began very early to instruct their daughters in the tasks they would eventually perform. Mothers, aunts, and grandmothers took them along when they gathered seeds and berries, cut stalks for weaving baskets, and tanned buckskin, and they encouraged even small girls to help with carrying water or wood. They fostered the diligence and skill expected of a woman. Although the lesson of lifelong obedience to duty was important for both sexes, it was emphasized for girls.

Female relationships were governed by the social structure of the Ndee extended family. Girls were close to their sisters, who would make the life journey with them; their brothers, once grown and married, would live far from them in other camps. As a girl approached adolescence, care was taken that she not spend unaccompanied time with her brothers at all; if a boy returned to the wickiup and found his sister alone there, he busied himself outside until others arrived. Girls were aware of all cousin and clan relationships, since marriage within the extended family was forbidden. Even today, Apache women do not marry men to whom they are at all related, and teenagers know these relationships intricately, as a matter of course.

One of the closest of ties existed between a girl and her maternal aunt, her mother's sister. If her mother died, this woman would raise her; if the aunt was not married, she might well become her stepmother, since widowed men frequently married the dead wife's sister. Men who took additional wives often chose the wife's sister as well. Aunts were expected to play a special part in preparing the girl for adulthood, for instance in making the special preparations for her Changing Woman ceremony.

As for uncles, there was a special dividend for nieces and nephews in adult brother-sister avoidance: an unmarried brother could show familial love toward his sister with proper decorum mainly by affection demonstrated to her children. There was also a special closeness to maternal grandparents, who spent more time with children than anyone other than the mother. They provided care when a mother's food-gathering and a father's hunting duties kept them away from the wickiup. If a widowed father could not find a new wife in the camp, a child would be reared by these grandparents.[6]

A girl's father was somewhat shut out of the full spectrum of family ties, because he was not permitted any relationship at all with his wife's mother. The practice of mother-in-law avoidance did not extend to his father-in-law, but this scene involving a nine-year-old girl, her maternal grandfather, and her father illustrates the special nature of relationships on the mother's side of the family:

*One day she came down to where her grandfather and her father were sitting together under the ramada. She was whistling. . . . Her grandfather said, "You should not whistle. Only boys whistle. You act like a boy." He said this in a teasing way because it is not considered proper for girls and women to whistle. But the girl, after waiting a minute or two, retorted in a quiet but determined voice, "You have many wrinkles in your neck." All the old man could do was laugh and make an exclamation of surprise. . . . Nothing more was done about it. The girl's father did not smile or say anything.* [7]

As the story about the girl and her whistling shows, an older girl was expected to change her demeanor, to make it more demure. Her hair no longer streamed heedlessly down her back; it was groomed and tied back with a large buckskin barrette when she was about ten years old, in a style she would wear until marriage, when she could once again loosen her hair over her shoulders. She took care not to expose herself in any way, sitting with her knees together. Serious responsibilities set in: she minded younger children, and attempted more-complex household chores. She learned the steps in making cakes of mescal, studied the food and medicinal qualities of plants, and made her first baskets and jars. Childhood's end approached with the coming of her first menstruation and her dance.

## Childhood: The Last One Hundred Years

*NARCISSUS DUFFY GAYTON:*
*MESCALERO RESERVATION, NEW MEXICO*
Narcissus Duffy was born in 1924 on the Mescalero Reservation in south-central New Mexico. She is the granddaughter of Victorio's granddaughter Beshad'è, who raised her when her mother died at the age of just twenty-seven. Victorio's descendants had lived in detention in Florida and Alabama, then at Fort Sill in Oklahoma, and finally among the Mescalero.

Narcissus's mother, Christine Kozine Duffy, had been

*In a photograph from an earlier time, older girls are seen
watching their younger brothers and sisters.*

born in a house in Fort Sill, not in a wickiup, and attended the Dutch Reformed church and the mission school
there. She was an "assimilated" Apache, who wore
middy blouses and black laced boots with her skirts, and
she groomed her hair in a modern style. Still, she
removed all the hairs from her brush, bound them and
burned them in the old way, so that no witch might find
a strand and bewitch her. She sought the best of both the
old and the new ways for her daughter:

> *Christine was concerned about the education of
> her daughter. She wanted Narcissus to know and
> have the best of white culture; at the same time
> she wanted her to be a proper Apache. The girl
> must know her genealogy. She must know the
> proper word to use for every relative; how each
> one was to be treated; how to show respect, what
> the obligations were.*[8]

When Christine died, the role of tradition became more
important in Narcissus's life, since her grandmother
Beshad'è[*] was now in charge. The rites of mourning for
her mother taught little Narcissus about the proper way to
grieve: her mother's possessions, her bedding, and even her
gramophone were destroyed, except for the few items that
were buried with her, like the buckskin dress she wore
when she had become White Painted Woman. Narcissus'
short hair was trimmed, and the ends tied up and hidden
in a tree deep in the forest. A ritual was held four nights in
succession, to chase her mother's ghost from the house.
Narcissus could never say her mother's name or call to her,
or her ghost might come to claim the daughter.[9]

After her mother's death, seven-year-old Narcissus

[*] Beshad'è means "beside or near her" or "stand beside her."

74

did not finish out the school year at the government boarding school on the reservation, where she had been sent that fall. She and her younger brother, Wendell, went to live with Beshad'è, while her father, Tom, remained close by. There were elaborate arrangements to be made, so that her father and Beshad'è, his mother-in-law, whom by custom he had to avoid, could share in family life. Narcissus brought the meals her grandmother cooked to Tom; when Beshad'è and her son-in-law took the car to Alamogordo or Tularosa to shop, a bedspread was hung to curtain off the back seat for the old woman. Upon arrival, the children watched their father walk out of sight before the grandmother emerged to do her errands.[10]

Grandmother told Narcissus the tales of Coyote, and warned Wendell and Narcissus to line up their shoes carefully facing east under their beds. They must not accidentally put their shoes on the wrong feet, for their feet would then resemble those of Bear, and bring Bear's bad influence to the home. Narcissus played with home-made rag dolls, shoe-box wagons, little wickiups made of grass, and improvised slingshots. From her grandmother she learned to do firewood and water chores, to gather nuts and cook, and to make buckskin in the traditional way. As she got older, Beshad'è instructed her not to sit on her brother Wendell's bed or use his possessions, and Narcissus learned to sit modestly, as an Apache young lady must.

Narcissus returned in the autumn after her mother's death to the Mescalero Agency Boarding School; later, she attended the White Tail Day School. The school regimens were strict, and she spoke only English and attended church services. She was, as her mother had hoped, a girl who had absorbed the ways of the white society; more than her mother could have anticipated, she had also experienced a traditional childhood with Beshad'è.

## GLADYS ETHELBAH LAVENDER:
## FORT APACHE RESERVATION, ARIZONA

Gladys Lavender, now in her seventies, has been a nurse and community health expert, and had legal training and served as a judge. She grew up on the Fort Apache Reservation with four brothers and three sisters in a wickiup no bigger than the living room of her house today. She fetched water from the river and wood for the fire; at the fireside, she heard the stories of the Coyote, the Fox, and the Snake. She slept on the floor. "In the wickiup I didn't feel cold. Now that I am old, every crack in the window bothers me."

Gladys and her sisters played house together, making tiny wickiups and bread out of mud, and they staged little Sunrise Dances for themselves. Then, when Gladys turned six, her parents brought her to Theodore Roosevelt Boarding School at Fort Apache. Her hair was cut, and a uniform replaced her camp dress. She knew not a word of English. Her sister Helen slept beside her, and taught her "yes" and "no" the first night. If you spoke Apache, you couldn't play in the gym on Saturdays, and sometimes you were strapped with a leather belt.

Gladys remembers that her father sang songs before he went hunting. He carried no money in his pocket, and if he took food along it was just eggs and potatoes, no meat. He could not talk about girls, and he could not waste anything he killed. When he returned with deer, her mother made buckskin and the family shared the meat with relatives and neighbors. "This is the way you are supposed to share," she says. She knows how to prepare buckskin, and it distresses her to see discarded deer carcasses in the dump. "Women don't know how anymore. Girls should learn to make and sew the skins." Gladys can still recall what she was taught to do as a girl: she could sew and bead a ceremonial dress, make a cradleboard, and weave baskets.

Gladys's father was a medicine man, and as a child she saw him sing many ceremonies. Her mother was a midwife; she sent her husband to get grass to place on the beds in more-modern homes at childbirth. She would say to the mother in labor, "This baby will be born like you, on the grass."

"Stay with your culture," she tells young people. "Listen to the elders who still know."

### TODAY: WHITERIVER ELEMENTARY SCHOOL, FORT APACHE RESERVATION

The generations of Narcissus and Gladys, for whom school days held pain as well as pleasure, have passed. Apache girls have surely made transitions, and the educational institutions on the reservations have changed also.

The girls who attend Whiteriver Elementary School on the Fort Apache Reservation are fortunate. Their campus is an award-winning school, cited for its model programs and promising practices. "These kids are wonderful," says Principal Myrna Hillyard.

Myrna Guenther Hillyard was born into a family that has served the Western Apache for over eighty years. She is the youngest of the nine children of Reverend Edgar Guenther and his wife, Minnie, who came to the reservation as Lutheran missionaries in 1911. The Guenthers started and ran with their own labor a school and an orphanage, as well as the congregation which still stands in Whiteriver. This account of their first schoolroom shows the educational tradition Myrna Hillyard has inherited:

> There were still no furnishings for the school. The Guenthers borrowed a buckboard and drove it twenty miles to the nearest sawmill, where they were given a load of scrap lumber. Back home at East Fork, Edgar Guenther worked until the wee

*hours of the morning fashioning the rough lum-*
*ber into desks and chairs, while Minnie sat at the*
*Oliver typewriter and pounded out school*
*lessons, being careful to use only examples and*
*illustrations that were familiar to the Apache chil-*
*dren.*

*The school opened in September and by*
*Christmas the students could carry on simple*
*English conversations and the Guenthers had*
*learned the corresponding Apache. The school*
*had proven to be an overwhelming success. Never*
*again did the missionaries have to solicit students,*
*for the Apache parents came to appreciate not*
*only the education, but also the love their chil-*
*dren were receiving.*[11]

Myrna Hillyard's Whiteriver Elementary is part of the
large Arizona public school system, but it also bears the
stamp of love, personal care, and commitment to Apache
children. She has brought to the campus the latest effec-
tive curricula and techniques.

Most students at the school begin their formal education in the Headstart Program for school readiness,
which enrolls over two hundred children in the center of
the town. When they enter kindergarten, they begin six
years of integrated whole-language learning that is based
on literature and supported by technology. The award-
winning parent-involvement program helps parents to
plan reading with children, and to reinforce their number
skills and encourage their natural curiosity in the course
of errands or housekeeping. Parent support and student
attendance rates are both high.

Every classroom has a computer, and each class is frequently scheduled into the Macintosh Lab adjacent to the
school's Media Center, a huge airy room filled with
books, tapes, and photo murals of Ndee traditional life.

Children publish their work constantly on the computers, and it fills the walls of the lab.

There is a large extended-day program after class hours. The clubs in art, photography, and traditional dance are particularly outstanding. The children's art has been reprinted and sold at the Heard Museum in Phoenix, and they develop their own photographs in the darkroom on campus. Jeannette Goseyun enjoyed particularly the Apache dance group, which performs for the public as well as the school.

A Cultural Awareness Program was inaugurated several years ago. Each class hangs tribal culture projects and murals in a colorful display in the cafeteria. Many of the children, raised with television and VCRs, do not speak Apache very well. There are two Apache-language teachers, Sherry Altaha and Edgar Perry of the Apache Cultural Center, and Apache is taught to all nine hundred students. "Ironically, this fulfills our foreign-language requirement from the state." Myrna Hillyard laughs. She adds seriously, "If you lose your language, you lose your culture. Written languages can last in books, but Apache is mainly a spoken language, and if it dies, it will truly be lost. That just must not happen." This belief is a long journey from the practices of the boarding and day schools of living memory, which disciplined children harshly for speaking their language and honoring the ways of their ancestors.

# ≈5≈
# Young Woman- hood

*I see that girl again,*
*Then I become like this;*
*I see my own sweetheart again,*
*Then I become like this.*

*Maiden, you talk kindly to me,*
*You, I shall surely remember it,*
*I shall surely remember you alone,*
*Your words are so kind,*
*You, I shall surely remember it.*[1]

## Young Womanhood: The Old Times

Once a girl was of age to marry, her thoughts focused on finding a life partner while she practiced with her mother the skills that would make her an excellent wife. Most girls were given in marriage between the ages of sixteen and eighteen, while men were older, in at least their early twenties. Between *Na'i'es* and wifehood lay a brief space of four or five years, which women thought of as the most lighthearted and enjoyable of their lives. Although many family considerations entered into the couples' choices, not the least of these was love. Falling in love, courtship, the early years of marriage: in any society, these are years cherished in memory.

There was never any doubt that all girls would marry:

> *Marriage was essential for the mature man or woman. Its importance is well indicated in folk tales where incidents relating to it are unduly stressed. A man without a wife was only half socially and economically potent. He had no one to cook for him, no one to bear him children, no one to gather and prepare wild foods and agricultural products, and he was therefore greatly to be pitied. The same was true of a woman without a husband, for she had no one to hunt for her, no one to bring her horses, and no one to give her children. It was said that men and women could not get along without each other.*[2]

Still, there were obstacles to the process of pairing off. A girl could not marry any man to whom she was even distantly related. Very rarely cousins did marry, but it was believed that the husband or wife would come to an untimely death and that their children would be sickly. Of course, the instances where such consequences did ensue were the only ones elders remembered. They solemnly related these to young people, so that they would avoid such mistakes themselves. Apache maidens carried in their heads detailed family trees; if a girl was approached in the semi-darkness at a dance by an improper partner, she would remind him: "I cannot dance with you—we are related."

An aunt or grandmother accompanied a girl to social

dances, so that she could help the girl to gravitate toward appropriate young men from other families who were in good standing in the community. Relatives guided such choices watchfully, since girls' marriages were the way a family acquired its male hunters and warriors. "A family's security thus rested on its ability and reputation in producing marriageable girls of good character. . . . "[3]

A greater obstacle was the acute shyness of teenagers of both sexes, which usually set in at adolescence and lasted well into young adulthood. The maiden or *na'i Liin*, as she was called from puberty until she married, did not dare to look a young man directly in the face; girls and boys avoided errands that would bring them into the company of young people of the opposite sex, and self-consciousness tied their tongues. In mixed company, they never excused themselves to go into the brush when nature called, or scratched themselves; girls had trouble eating in front of boys. Adults teased them mercilessly.

There were mortifying accounts of boys who were caught relieving themselves. If girls and boys met in a work group, it was an unlucky person who had not planned ahead; it was an embarrassment just to need a drink of water while laboring in the heat of the afternoon.

A girl could maintain a natural relationship with only a select few boys in her circle: these were her "cross-cousins," the sons of her mother's brother or her father's sister. With these boys, she had the happy relief of normal conversation, and a unique teasing and confiding relationship as well. When young adults took a liking to one another, cross-cousins facilitated their hesitant initial steps. For instance, a girl's cross-cousin might suggest to a boy that the two of them help a group of girls harvesting corn, knowing that she would be one of the girls in the cornfield. A meeting out on a path could involve a girl with her boy cross-cousin and a boy with his girl cross-cousin. Conversation would be easier that way; the best of all situations developed if the accompanying cross-cousins started to like one another too.

A young man who wished to engage the attentions of a girl resorted to careful strategies. He could hide near a path he knew she used, and throw stones near her feet; older women today recall the throwing of pebbles as the first sign of interest evinced by their future husbands. Girls had their tactics also. Bolder girls sometimes laughed with their girlfriends in voices loud enough for youths to hear. They even spoke to the boys, perhaps admiring an object a boy had made and requesting that he make one for her.

The best method for beginning a relationship was the one Apache society had clearly set up for courtship— partner dancing at ceremonial events. Girls asked boys to dance, and many kept the same partners all evening. The all-night dances brought young people together at a romantic moonlit time, when special songs of love and longing were being sung; lyrics like the one at the beginning of this chapter were apt to bring out sentimental feelings. "The morning songs, the love songs, sound beautiful. They are high pitched. We like them best of all. People just fall in love there singing them."[4]

This paired dancing was also performed with discretion; no Apache youth could kiss a girl in public or embrace her closely. Young men never spoke to one another about women's body parts; those who did were considered vulgar and unpleasant. There were ideals of beauty sought in both men and women, although they may not have been voiced because of modesty. A girl considered pretty was of medium height and weight, buxom, with an oval face and small features. Large hands and feet were thought ugly for both men and women, and long, well-kept hair were admired on both. Girls bound

83

*Young Apache girls of an earlier time*

their hair at the neck like the two girls in the photograph, wearing their good camp dresses and jewelry. An attractive man had an open, smiling face, a lean body, and erect posture.[5]

The character and personality of an ideal Apache partner were more important than looks or present prosperity. The best husbands and wives were cheerful, to get along with all the members of the extended family; strong, to endure the hard life ahead; and hardworking, to provide for the children and the elders who would be their responsibility.

Women's virginity held the highest value, although a woman who was "spoiled" through premarital experience, divorce, or widowhood could still find a husband, especially if she was attractive. However, the marriage gifts given for her were much diminished. Girls who lost their virginity could be whipped with a rope or stick, perhaps in public, to provide a lesson to other girls who listened, watched, and guarded their own purity.[6] After a battle or raid, the elation of the victory party with the drinking of much *tulkbai,* corn liquor, could lead to "night crawling"; a girl had to beware of young warriors creeping into her wickiup to lie with her.[7]

The Apache belief in witchcraft extended also to affairs of the heart. Older men, from whose ranks many witches came, were especially suspected of using spells to make girls fall in love with them. Even though an adolescent girl's hair was kept bound up, if such a man got hold of a hair from her head, he might bewitch her into falling for him.

However tentative and careful love relationships had to be, eventually a mutual commitment was established. Just to make sure he was reading signals properly, a boy sometimes left meat or game he had caught at the entrance to a girl's wickiup; if she wished to have him, she would cook and use it, bringing some to the boy's wickiup. If women from a girl's family brought food to a boy's home and he did not want her, the food remained untouched outside the wickiup. There were ways to know.

The next move belonged to the young man's family. His relatives or representatives came to the wickiup of his bride-to-be, and offered gifts to the girl's family, perhaps three horses with saddles and blankets (or a number of head of cattle in later reservation times). The marriage gifts were critical. A young man had to wait for marriage until he and his family had enough horses; thus raids to acquire them were sometimes staged.

Little formality marked the marriage itself. After the families shared food, the couple moved into their own wickiup, built by the new wife near her parents' home. For the first weeks of the marriage, the bride fetched a portion of the meals her mother cooked, to feed the two of them. It was difficult for them to eat in each other's presence:

> *After they had been married for some time they might recall their embarrassment with some amusement: "I never thought I could bear to have you watch me while I ate, but here we are looking at each other and chewing at the same time. We used to be so self-conscious that, when lice bit us on the legs or head, we let them bite, not daring to scratch.*[8]

One of the signs that the marriage had matured a bit appeared when the bride's mother told her it was time to cook for her own husband.

It took several nights before the young couple slept alone together and could consummate their marriage.

*An old photograph shows an Apache bride and bridegroom.*

Often cousins slept between them at first: the new husband slept on one side, then came his male cousin, followed by her female cousin and finally the young wife. The cousins arranged tactfully after a few nights to slip away and leave the couple by themselves to make love for the first time. Understandably, overcoming shyness and inexperience was difficult. Apache parents did not explain sex to their children, and although young people had surely watched animals and knew generally what lovemaking entailed, they were after all a couple who had trouble even eating in each other's presence.

An Apache husband found his whole world changed and filled with new and exacting responsibilities and relationships. His duties were tied to the needs of his wife's family, whose camp he served. However, he had absolutely no contact with his mother-in-law, who made many of the decisions affecting him: never could he see her or speak to her. Probably the Ndee had discovered long ago that in avoiding this common source of discord in domestic arrangements, everyone's lives ran more smoothly. Mother-in-law avoidance was in no way comical, but done in serious respect and deference to the wife's mother. Roles and duties seemed easier for the young wife, who remained among familiar expectations and people she loved.

Sometimes status or economic considerations resulted in a match that was not initiated by the couple at all, and then there might be complications in establishing new relationships. Girls' families occasionally arranged marriages for them with virtual strangers from families willing to pay for wives with many horses or cattle. Chiefs' daughters commonly married the sons of chiefs from other clans or outstanding warriors, men they barely knew. This happened to Victorio's daughter Dilth Cleyhen. She had twice married men she chose and was widowed each time, both husbands shot down in raids. Her first husband was the father of her daughter Beshad'è, and the second husband died while Dilth Cleyhen was pregnant with another daughter. In 1873, her father, Victorio, came to her and said:

> *"A great man has asked to marry you. He has brought me horses."*
> *Dilth Cleyhen asked, "Yes, who is this man?" Within her heart she knew and she was pleased. It was Carl Mangas, the son of the great chief, Mangas Coloradas.*
> *Carl Mangas, two years Dilth Cleyhen's senior, was not huge like his father. He was a kind man with a broad smile and a general philosophy of peace. He would make a good husband and father. He hunted well. Dilth Cleyhen's memories took her back to the days of her Puberty Feast when she remembered the tall, gangly teenager who sometimes accompanied Red Sleeves.*
> *"I agree to marry him," she told her father. Later she expressed reservations, not enough to cancel the agreement, but one problem in particular that rankled. She would be Mangas's second wife. He was married to a woman named Huera, a real troublemaker. . . .* [9]

Most men had only one wife, but men of eminence or prosperity might marry four or five times. In his lifetime, Geronimo married nine women, although not all were alive at once. After the first marriage, following wives were frequently chosen from among the sisters and cousins of the first wife; in-law obligations were complicated, and arrangements were easier if there was just one family to whom a husband was beholden. This pattern is called *sororal polygyny*, multiple marriage to sisters. The Ndee managed the pattern with equanimity: separate but

*Schuma with his two wives; a photograph from 1888.*

nearby wickiups were usually maintained, and the children of another wife were treated almost as warmly as one's own, especially if death or circumstance required the raising of nieces and nephews. Later, when Christian missionaries began the conversion of the Apache, men with more than one wife faced terrible choices. "When the husband was ready to accept Christianity and was informed that he must choose one wife and her children and abandon the rest, the minister's task was a discouraging one. How could a woman and children exist without protection and support?"[10]

Once an Apache woman married and childbearing began, the easy days of young womanhood were over. On her shoulders fell the day-to-day maintenance of her extended family's diet and health and happiness. She welcomed these responsibilities to her kin with cheerful and unrelenting effort, and with prayers that no evil spirit should come their way to bring harm to the world she built for them.

## Young Womanhood: The Last One Hundred Years

Once the Apache resistance ended and resettlement on the reservations was complete, most adolescent girls were enrolled in boarding and day schools set up on reservations. This caused heartbreak for parents. The children at Fort Sill were sent to a boarding school thirty miles away at Anadarko; their parents, still prisoners, had no horses and made trips on foot to see them. Some girls were sent to all-Indian boarding institutions as far away as Pennsylvania. These schools' objectives for young women were to make them into "proper" English-speaking Anglo-style homemakers.

Paula Gunn Allen, a Laguna/Sioux literary scholar, wrote of her great-grandmother's education in the Indian boarding schools:

*Schools that were little more than concentration camps for young people were erected all over the West, Midwest, and even in the East, where the star colonial establishment, Carlisle Indian School, was located. My great-grandmother got her education there. She learned how to be a literate, modest, excruciatingly exacting maid for well-to-do white farmers' and ranchers' wives. She didn't follow exactly the course laid out for her, and became the farmer-rancher's wife instead. The bitter fruits of her efforts are still being eaten by her grandchildren, great-grandchildren, and great-great-grandchildren. I often wonder if we will recover from the poisonous effects of Indian-saving.* [11]

This grim experience was shared by many Apache girls too. Still, some girls grew up into leadership roles that transcended the efficient homemaker slots envisioned for them; these women, like Mildred Cleghorn, welcomed the chance to start their educations in the boarding schools.

## RAMONA CHIHUAHUA :
## CARLISLE BARRACKS SCHOOL, PENNSYLVANIA

It was 1886, and the Apache Wars were over. The remnant of Geronimo's band was shipped by train to Florida, but the children were sent to the Carlisle Barracks School near Harrisburg, Pennsylvania, where the first Indian school outside the reservations had been started in 1879. Daklugie,[*] the son of Juh, and Ramona, the daughter of Chihuahua, were among them. Neither one knew where they were being sent, or to what fate. Ramona asked Daklugie, who had a small but sharp knife, if he would

[*] "the one who shaked"

kill her if she were attacked. They were in fact to join other Indians from around the United States in learning elementary school subjects, farming and shop skills for the boys, housekeeping for the girls, and most importantly, how to use English and obtain the habits and appearance of non-Indians.

Daklugie told historian Eve Ball:

> *The next day the torture began. The first thing they did was cut our hair. I had taken my knife from one of my long braids and wrapped it in my blankets, so I didn't lose it. But I lost my hair. And without it how would Usin recognize me when I went to the Happy Place?*
> *. . . Learning English wasn't too bad. There was a necessity for memorizing everything because we could neither read nor write. Before the winter was over I was learning to read. My teacher was a white lady and she was very patient and kind to us. She taught us to write, too, and she was not bossy as most white ladies are. She was polite. She seemed to know without being told that I wanted desperately to be able to read and she helped me.*[12]

However, even the teachers who were kind caused difficulties for the Apache students, for whom being shamed before others was the worst punishment. When Daklugie innocently misused an English word, his teacher became angry and told him to remain after the others left to write a sentence using the word properly a hundred times.

The Carlisle students spent their summers in the homes of Pennsylvania Dutch farmers near the school. Girls like Ramona were taught to keep house as the farmwives did, to plant gardens and can their harvests, sew

*Jack and Kesseta, captured in New Mexico and sent to Carlisle Barracks School in Pennsylvania in 1887.*

Anglo-style clothes, and make butter. How strange it must have seemed to the girls, who had learned from their mothers and grandmothers to gather and process wild foods, to tan and sew buckskin, and to make baskets and build wickiups. As always, they were diligent and obedient, and they learned. When Ramona Chihuahua and "Asa" Daklugie, as he was named at Carlisle, were married eight years later at Fort Sill, Oklahoma, Ramona and her mother made a lovely beaded buckskin wedding dress, but she also sewed a silk Victorian-style wedding gown. They had two separate wedding ceremonies. Ramona was buried in the buckskin wedding dress.[13]

## MILDRED IMACH CLEGHORN: FORT SILL, OKLAHOMA

Mildred Imach was born in 1910 at Fort Sill, Oklahoma, the daughter of Apache prisoners of war there. She was a graduate of the Indian school in Lawrence, Kansas, called the Haskell Institute. Her mother, who had attended an Indian boarding school herself, preferred that she go to a public school: "I don't want any child of mine going to a boarding school," she said. Mildred graduated from Haskell and then earned a college degree in home economics. Her ambition was to become an extension agent, helping reservation families. She worked for a year and a half as a teacher at the Riverside School, an Indian educational institution in Oklahoma.

> "We had a cottage department at Riverside," she remembered. "One of the most wonderful opportunities our Indian children ever had was being in cottages because we created a home life situation. There were twenty-two students, eleven boys and eleven girls from all tribes. Navajos, people from the North, and everywhere. . . . It was just one big family and each child had work to do. So,

*they learned how to keep house, how to cook,
how to do the laundry, how to do everything. . . .
Then we had study hours. I think it was the most
wonderful thing that could have happened. Today
I get graduation notices from the grandchildren
of the children I taught, which is amazing to
me."[14]*

Mildred's mother had encouraged her to go to school, learn the white man's way, and fight for what she wanted. "I'm still fighting because we have a good way. I mean, the quality of life that the old folks lived was beautiful. It was loving and sharing, and what else can you ask?"[15]

In the PBS documentary "Geronimo and the Apache Resistance," this striking and compelling woman helped to narrate the story of the wars, the surrender and captivity of her Chiricahua forebears. Nothing in her boarding-school adolescence had taken from her the Apache identity she treasures and a forthright leadership style she shares with other female tribal leaders.

Mildred Imach served as an extension agent in Kansas and Oklahoma. She married Bill Cleghorn in the Reformed Church on the Mescalero Reservation in New Mexico, and ultimately became the tribal chair of the Fort Sill Apache Tribe. Mildred Imach Cleghorn was selected 1989 Indian of the Year.

## JEANETTE GOSEYUN AND EDITH HARVEY: WHITERIVER, ARIZONA, TODAY

Jeanette Dan Goseyun was born on August 16, 1979, in Phoenix, just eleven months after the birth of her sister Carla. Her first name came from her great aunt Jeanette, the sister of her maternal grandfather. Everyone on her father's side shares the middle name, Dan. As she relates the background of her name, she swings the ninety-five

96

*Jeanette Goseyun with the Scholar-Athlete trophy*

African-style braids she has put into her hair the day before, just for fun. She is wearing shorts and a long T-shirt, white socks and black Birkenstock-type sandals. She looks nothing like the Apache maiden Jeanette on the cover of this book.

Jeannette and her family moved back to Whiteriver when she was small, and the town is the only home she can remember. She has spoken English all her life, although she does know some Apache. She was always an outstanding student and athlete from her earliest school days at Whiteriver Elementary School. In the photograph, Jeanette holds the Whiteriver Middle School Scholar Athlete award, which she won at the end of her eighth-grade year. She was a Student Council member, an honor student at the middle school, and excelled at basketball and volleyball, and she now competes in those sports at Alchesay High School.

Jeanette says that she always wanted a Sunrise Dance from the time that she was small. She never recalls it as a choice she made, but as a privilege she anticipated happily. She did not really have to learn the steps she performed, because she had acquired them through watching her sisters' dances and those of many others, and by participating in performance groups all through grade school. The little Goseyun girls wore camp dresses and traditional jewelry for their childhood portraits, which hang on the living-room walls. Little girls at the White-river dances dress just like small Carmen, Carla, and Jeanette in those photographs, their outfits complete down to the turned-up toes of their small knee-high moccasins. The Apache tradition of the Changing Woman Ceremony belonged to Jeanette before she even thought about it.

It is believed that the traits that a girl exhibits during her Sunrise Dance will characterize her from that time on, and this certainly seems true of Jeanette. Although she suffered throughout her ceremony with flu and a high fever, she never faltered through days and nights of continuous dancing; she doesn't give up in her pursuits and she attains her goals. Jeanette attended an academic enrichment program for Native Americans on the campus of the University of California at Davis during the summer of her fourteenth birthday. She was homesick at first and lonely without her hometown friends, and she thought of returning home to Arizona. She decided instead to stick to the program, and grew to enjoy it so much that she planned to return the next summer. When Jeanette entered high school as an outstanding mathematics student, she was placed in Algebra II, but soon had to rejoin most of her classmates in first-year Algebra. She studied hard and moved back up to the second-year class, which she completed successfully at the end of her first high school year. Persistence is the hallmark of Jeanette Goseyun.

&

Edith Harvey, twenty-one years old, works in the Tribal Education Office during college holidays. She is studying to be a registered nurse at Fort Lewis College in Durango, Colorado. She has two younger sisters, Verlene, eighteen, also attending Fort Lewis, and Melenda, sixteen. Fort Lewis provides full scholarships for Indian students,

98

*Edith Harvey*

and many Whiteriver girls continue their education there after graduation from Alchesay High School. Edith was a student assistant to the school nurse, who took a special interest in her future career.

Her mother, Betty Harvey, holds a two-year degree from the Haskell Institute, and works for the White Mountain Apache Tribe in the food-distribution office. She has been divorced for eleven years, and has stressed to her daughters the im-portance of independence and training for the future. Edith's mother did not expect her to marry early, but rather to complete her education. Delayed marriage is common in Edith's circle; only one of her friends has already wed.

Edith wants to work as a hospital nurse when she graduates, and then to enter the Peace Corps. Her female role models are Tribal Council member Judy DeHose and her grandmother Villie Nagle, who is almost eighty years old and lives with her daughter and grandchildren. "She's really strong, and young at heart," says Edith. She also encourages Edith's ambitions. "Once you have earned that degree, nothing can take it from you," her grandmother tells her. "No matter what anybody says, it's what you believe that counts."

Mr. Ensman, Edith's high school biology teacher, has been an important influence in Edith's life. Many of the girls at Alchesay who excel academically are particularly outstanding in math and science, which is not typical of American girls throughout the country.

Although Edith did not have a Sunrise Dance, there have been many traditional elements in her upbringing. She has a godmother, Jennifer Barahas, who massaged her in a brief rite soon after she came of age. She has attended many Sunrise Dances, including those of Carmen and Carla Goseyun. Of the stories she was told as a child, she remembers best that of the old woman with the burning burden basket who came to take away children who misbehaved; someday she hopes to repeat the stories to her own children. What does she aspire to over the next decade? Edith replied that she wished for a rewarding nursing job, a good husband, and "five or six children."

Edith was also asked to complete the sentence "To me, being Apache means . . . " She took the question very seriously and thought for a few moments. "The greatest honor," she said quietly.

## ≈6≈
# Adult-
# hood

*I come to White Painted Woman,*
*By means of long life I come to her.*
*I come to her by means of her blessing,*
*I come to her by means of her good fortune,*
*I come to her by means of all her different fruits;*
*By means of the long life she bestows, I come to*
*her;*
*By means of this holy truth she goes about.*[1]

The agave, or century plant, blooms and bears its edible
stalk only after twenty years of growth; women
processed and baked these stalks into cakes of "mescal,"
the staple plant food of the Ndee. A mature wife, *isdzán*
was like the agave; after some twenty years of childhood
and young womanhood, she bore children and sustained
her family by harvesting the bounty of the land. Women
built the physical shelter of the home and maintained the
spiritual shelter of the family with faithful nurturing.

# Adulthood: The Old Times

The Ndee had no permanent camps or villages. They were always on the move to gather edible plants as they came into season, to follow the herds they hunted, and to stage raids into Old Mexico for livestock or horses. Each band had its own set of hunting and gathering areas, which it would revisit in a varying circuit; during some years, a woman came again to the spot where she was born, and there were special prayers to be said there. The women knew where they had left caches of food: baskets, jars of seeds, nuts, and dried meats they had buried in earlier years. They were acutely sensitive to patterns that would tell them when to visit a valley that would be rich with berries or a site where the mescal stalks would be ready to harvest.

*"Let's go east, closer to the Muddy River, the Rio Grande," the women counseled their husbands. "There's lots of mesquite all the way from east of the Magdalena Mountains south to where the river heads north. Let's camp there. I'm hungry for mesquite." And when the beans were gathered, some were stewed with deer or antelope meat or just boiled, forming a thick, sweet gruel. Any excess was ground on a metate and stored for future use.*

*During the late summer months, in the foothills below the rise of the Peloncillos and Animas Mountains, the red fruit of the three-leaved sumac ripened and provided succulent fare, especially when dried and mixed with mescal gathered late the next spring. . . .*

*"The weather is getting warm. Already we've gathered the stalks of the narrow-leafed yucca and roasted the thick ones, sun-drying them for*

*times when we are hungry. Now, we must think about a longer trip—one where we find the big mescal."*[2]

The harvest and processing of mescal was an extended project. The women used a chisel-like wooden wedge to pry the center stalks out of the plants, and then stripped away the leaves. The trimmed plants were baked for two days in a deep, wide pit lined with stones and smoldering wood; each woman cut her mark into her particular stalks and offered prayers over the pit, which was then covered with earth. When the baked mescal was dug up, it was pounded into a pulp, shaped into large flat slabs, and dried on frames. They cut the mescal into cakes of dry food that could keep indefinitely, to which they added water, fresh nuts, or berries to make a nourishing gruel to serve to husbands and children. Women ate last, from the remains of the family's meal; nothing was ever wasted.

The women depended on unusual allies in the gathering of piñon nuts:

*We began our harvest of piñons by finding trails of pack rats and tracking them to their dens. The nests were sometimes two and a half feet high and about that in diameter. Sometimes we got as many as two gallons or more of the tiny nuts from one cache. The rats never carry a faulty piñon to their hoard. When we could find no more nests, we placed skins under the trees and beat the lower limbs with clubs; and we even picked up some one by one.*[3]

The diet of the Western Apache in Arizona was about two-thirds plant foods. The staples were mescal, sahuaro fruit, acorns, mesquite beans, fruit of Spanish bayonet, sunflower seeds, fruit of prickly pear, piñon nuts, and juniper berries, with the mescal and acorns the most important.[4] Acorn meal mixed with dried meat and fat and then rolled into balls made a portable meal for raiders or warriors on horseback. The Apache also farmed small fields of corn, along with some beans and squash. The corn was planted in the spring; after summer forays for wild foods, the people returned in the fall to harvest the cornfields. The combination of foraging, farming, and hunting for both small and large game provided enough food, but no one supply alone could nourish them; the travel circuit was always necessary.

Hunting and raiding supplemented plant staples. The principal hunting season was late fall through winter, when plant foods were scarce; winter was also raiding time. Men never traveled far away from the camps on hunts; they butchered and dressed the meat and brought it quickly home for feasting and drying before any of it spoiled.

Preparing hides required long hours of labor. Women scraped away the flesh that clung to the hide from the inside of the skin; after days of soaking, the outside fur was scraped off. Drying followed, and then a tanning paste of fat and deer brains was worked into the skin. Pulling and stretching the softened hide took days of uninterrupted work.[5]

Once a woman had a good buckskin hide, she could cut it and sew it into moccasins and shirts and saddlebags. Blacktail deer leather made good moccasins, to which Western Apache women added turned-up tabs at the toes as protection from cactus spines on the desert floor. In the 1800s, buckskin clothing was mostly replaced by cloth; the Apache traded for colorful calico to make into shawls, shirts, and camp dresses, a modification of the Victorian dress styles they observed in Anglo women. They also acquired needles, thread, and Venetian glass beads from the Hispanic settlers.[6]

*The old method of preparing buckskin. The woman at the left had a large hide drying in front of her wickiup.*

The nomadic life allowed for few possessions, and those had to be light and portable. The women made some pottery. Widows and divorced women, the *bì-záhn*, who needed to exchange pots for food, were the most active potters. But pots were too heavy to use as the camps moved onward, and baskets were the best receptacles; they weighed little and they never broke in transport. Ndee women were suberb basket makers with several decorative and distinctive basket styles. There were baskets for carrying possessions, for seed parching, winnowing, food preparation, grain storage, serving, washing, and ceremonial uses. Some baskets were coated in

*An 1880 photograph shows a canvas-draped wickiup.*

*An Apache chief and his wife in front of
their permanent wickiup.*

*White Mountain Apache water carriers of about 1880*

piñon pitch to make the watertight *tús*, the Apache water carrier, which was fitted with a tumpline for transport.

Basketmaking was usually a winter project, taught by mothers, aunts, and grandmothers to younger girls. Women expressed themselves with artistry, working traditional symbols into exquisite and intricate designs. It is a denigration of Indian arts that they are less esteemed and called "crafts," just as Indian legends are "folklore" instead of literature; and Indian "song" is regarded as inferior to European-style music. Carolyn Niethammer might have had Apache baskets in mind when she wrote:

> *the early Indian woman wasn't inspired merely by the desire for lovely pots and baskets to use for gathering foods and serving meals; she also garnered a great deal of joy in the acts of conceiving new patterns and implementing her inspirations. The most rewarding aspects of handicrafts were often more psychological than material, yet because these early people had no time for "art for art's sake," such as paintings and sculpture, her talents had to be confined to the manufacture or decoration of useful items.*
>
> *A woman's talent for fine craftsmanship was usually rewarded by the respect she received from the other women—the real connoisseurs of handicrafts. While the finer details in the perfection of a skill might be scarcely apparent to an untutored eye, another craftswoman could see and appreciate ingenuity and true virtuosity.*[7]

Women built the home itself, and its tools and implements. The Apache shelter was called a *gowa* or wickiup; it could be constructed by an industrious woman in a single afternoon. Light, flexible poles of cottonwood or willow were bent to form a ribbed domed shape, with an

*This historical photograph shows a basket weaver in front of
a wickiup covered for protection by a wagon tarp.*

open eye in the top to allow smoke to escape from the fireplace below. Originally, the ribs were piled with a thatch of bear grass; later, canvas trade goods were draped over the poles on the windward side. A cluster of wickiups went up quickly as a band chose a temporary settlement. When reservation life demanded more-permanent settlements, refinements like lumber-framed entranceways appeared.

Women of the Ndee modified their work when they were pregnant. They wore maternity belts for abdominal support, made of the skins of deer, mountain lions, or antelope, all of whom gave birth to their young without difficulty. Expectant mothers avoided rough riding and lifting; they ate few fatty foods and no animal intestines, which were associated with stillbirths because of the umbilical cord that could strangle a baby. Helen Crocker, a twentieth-century midwife in Whiteriver, recommended walking—but not too far, and herbs to supplement the diet.

Some old wives' tales presage those heard in America today. It was bad luck to prepare clothing or other items for the new baby until it actually arrived. There were conditions of the pregnancy that indicated whether the woman carried a boy or a girl; if the skin across her nose freckled or discolored, it was a boy. When a nursing toddler became cranky, his mother could be pregnant again.

The Apache were strong believers in prenatal influence, so pregnant women observed social and psychological precautions. They took special care to be pleasant to all their neighbors; women would not risk antagonizing anyone who had the power to witch the growing infant. They did not attend ceremonies at which the Gaan would be present, or look directly at the moon. A pregnant woman who spent her term peacefully would bear a happy and healthy child.

Other women of her family, her grandmother, mother, and aunts, attended a woman giving birth. Naturally, her husband had to leave the wickiup, since he could not be in the presence of his mother-in-law. He also could not see the afterbirth, which might weaken men as did menstrual blood, which it resembled. A midwife was summoned, preferably one in the woman's own family. She helped the woman to kneel or stand with her hands tied around a wooden post, and massaged the abdomen downward. At delivery, she cut the umbilical cord with a sharp reed or yucca leaf. The midwife might even perform a cesarean delivery, sewing up the incision she had cut with horsetail stitches.

Long ago multiple births were feared by Apache women; they were considered signs of suspected adultery on the mother's part. Only one baby, the male if there was one, was permitted to live. Infants with harelips or other deformities were destroyed as well. In the early twentieth century, Reverend Edgar Guenther saved the life of an infant girl near Whiteriver:

> *Many relatives had gathered and were discussing the fate of a baby girl born with six fingers on each hand. The grandmother insisted she be killed immediately. Guenther, realizing the gravity of the situation, picked up a butcher knife, held it over the flames of the campfire, wiped it clean with his handkerchief, and then quickly cut off the infant's extra fingers. The parents immediately accepted the child as normal.*[8]

An Apache husband could mutilate an adulterous wife by slitting off the tip of her nose. Presumably, no man would desire a woman who had been thus disfigured. A man who left camp for a long period sometimes arranged for a friend to spy on his wife to assure her fidelity while he was gone. This agent, called *bà•sití* ("he lies beside it"), was often a woman, whose constant proximity to the wife aroused no suspicion.

Adultery was frequently addressed in Apache legends. Several stories about Coyote concern his promiscuous sexual behavior. Sometimes he emerged unscathed from his escapades, but his partners did not (teaching females to be wary of tempters); but usually Coyote also suffered the consequences of his behavior. In this story, the husband tortured Coyote to death:

> *He took out his gun and ran in there and caught them. He said, "All right. You two sit over there. . . . She is going to put four little rocks in the fire and let them get hot. She is going to dip them in tallow and you are going to eat them. If you live through that, you can have everything. I will leave and never come back." He told her, "Go on, heat those rocks. Hurry up!"*[9]

Since Coyote was a *di-yin*, he thought he could devour burning rocks and survive, but he was wrong. Now the vengeful husband turned to the woman. He took out his knife to cut off her nose, but she ran to her mother's wickiup, where he could never go, and hid.

There were times when a serious affair led to a husband murdering his wife. One of Geronimo's warriors, Fun, who had enlisted in the infantry while a prisoner in Alabama, attempted to kill his unfaithful young wife with a pistol. He then shot himself to death, preferring suicide to the punishment the army would surely inflict upon him. "Fun thought that he had killed his wife. He knew that the Apaches would approve, but he wanted to escape the terrible death and mutilation of hanging."[10]

113

This historical photograph shows an Apache woman who was
punished for adultery by the slitting of her nose.

A woman who knew that her husband was an adulterer had no way to exact revenge. If his behavior continued, she divorced him. There were many reasons for Apache divorce: "laziness, incompetence . . . failure of a man to observe respect and avoidance with his wife's kin and to help them as a son-in-law should, continual quarreling, maltreatment of a wife, jealousy, and infidelity."[11] Divorce was called *yo' nai ʞ t'eeh,* "they two wish to separate," a name which indicates that it was as frequently a wife's choice as a husband's. It was swiftly and easily accomplished. The wife left her husband's belongings outside the wickiup, and he was expected to take them away with him as he left her camp forever. A husband desiring a divorce could simply fail to return from a hunt or raid.

Divorced or widowed women, especially those with children, usually took another husband, but there were some who remained single. There was a place for them in society; the Apache took care of their own, and no band would leave a woman without protection. Some young men sought divorced women, welcoming their sexual experience and the smaller marriage gifts that were required for them.

As most marriages were made for love, widows felt their loss keenly. The most famous widow of the Ndee was given the name Gouyen, "Wise Woman," after she avenged the death of her husband herself instead of leaving it to the warriors to stage a raid of revenge.

Gouyen's husband had been slaughtered and scalped by a Comanche chief. She waited until the middle of the night, strapped onto her back the beaded buckskin dress she had worn in her Changing Woman ceremony, and stole out of her camp on foot. For three nights she followed the trail of the Comanche, steadily jogging in the characteristic gait that enabled the Apache to cover great distances without stopping, until the sun rose and she hid and rested in the shade.

On the fourth night, she spied the campfire of the Comanche, who were celebrating their victory with raucous dance and drink. Undetected, Gouyen stole the chief's black horse and tethered it in a distant thicket for her escape. Then she dressed in her beautiful ceremonial robes and approached the campfire. She walked up to the drunken chief, who wore her husband's scalp on his belt, and lured him into dancing with her, drawing him farther and farther from the firelight. She reached for his knife but failed to grasp it. The chief seized Gouyen. She sank her teeth into his neck and held on fiercely as his blood soaked her buckskins; finally, he fell dead at her feet. She cut out the chief's heart, scalped him, and took his breechclout and moccasins.

For three fevered days, Gouyen galloped back to her own camp on the black horse, wearing her bloodstained buckskin dress. When she returned, her father, Chief Peso, displayed the Comanche's garments to his band:

> *"My daughter," he said, "is a brave and good woman. She has done a braver thing than has any man among the Mescaleros. She has killed the Comanche chief; and she has brought his weapons and garments to her people. She has ridden his mount. Let her always be honored by my people.*
> *And let her name be Gouyen!*[12]

Gouyen was not the only Apache woman warrior. Many women accompanied their husbands on war raids. Most remained behind the battle lines to cook and nurse the wounded, but some handled weapons as well.[13] Women were skilled riders and made excellent scouts. Four women captured by the Mexicans and taken a thousand miles away to be servants in Mexico City escaped after six years, and walked all the way home. They lived off the land on their long trek, surviving a mountain-lion attack as well.[14]

The women of the Ndee were formidable. The tradition of their hard work and of their courage in adversity continues to the present day.

## Adulthood: The Last One Hundred Years

*LOZEN, WOMAN WARRIOR*
For two decades after the Civil War, one-quarter of the United States Cavalry was deployed in the Southwest, hunting down Apache bands that totaled just a few hundred fighters. The great chiefs Cochise and Mangas Coloradas had perished, Mangas at the hands of soldiers who decapitated him and boiled his head to obtain a "clean" skull to send east to the Smithsonian Institution. About five thousand United States troops and three thousand soldiers from Mexico roamed the territory of the Chiricahua, chasing Victorio's group and that of Naiche and his powerful medicine man Geronimo.

Victorio also had a companion with astounding spiritual power. She was his sister, Lozen, and her gift enabled her to find the enemy. This was so valuable to Victorio that he kept her at his side, despite the Apache tradition of brother-sister avoidance among mature siblings. Perhaps it was the violation of this tradition that kept the Apache from telling the Anglos about Lozen until many years after her death. It was difficult to explain this singular woman who traded marriage and childbearing for raiding and warfare, and her people did not want others to assume that she was a deviant or a curiosity. To them, she was, and she remains, a holy woman.

It was said that Lozen never married because she had fallen in love with an Indian stranger, a man from New York's Seneca tribe who scouted the Southwest in the 1860s, when the Seneca removal to the Plains was taking place. This mysterious stranger, whom some called "The Gray Ghost," left the Apacheria and was never seen again. Although Lozen had no husband and no child, she knew the Apache female skills well and she gathered food and built wickiups with the other women when she was not out with war or raiding parties.

Lozen had studied with medicine men and kept a sacred vigil to receive her power. When she used it to locate the enemy, she stood with her arms raised to the open sky and turned in a long slow circle, singing a prayer to Usin the Creator. She stopped circling when her palms began to tingle; sometimes the feeling was so strong that her palms turned purple. She knew the direction and even the distance of the enemy by the strength of the sensation in her hands.

Lozen's medicine power healed Victorio. When a bullet pierced his shoulder, she prayed over him. "She burned the thorns from a leaf of nopal, split it, and bound the fleshy side to the wound. The next day, I rode." Victorio proclaimed, "I depend on Lozen." She sat with the men in councils and war ceremonies. They acknowledged that she rode with the best of them, ran faster than most, and used her rifle and knife as well as they could. They had given her the name "Dextrous Horse Thief" when she was a girl; Lozen stole the horses that enabled Victorio's Warm Springs band to escape from the San Carlos Reservation in 1875. She took particular care of all the mounts, over the thousands of miles they traveled without proper food and water for horses or riders.

Comrades attested to Lozen's loyalty and courage. Once she crawled on her stomach through a barrage of shellfire to retrieve a sack of bullets dropped by a rider. She was far away, guiding a Mescalero woman back into New Mexico, when Victorio was slain by Mexican troops at Los Castillos in 1880, and many said that she would have detected the enemy and shielded her brother if she had been with him.

After Victorio's death, she rode with his surviving warriors to avenge the deaths at Los Castillos, and then she joined another band. Its leaders were Naiche and Geronimo, and it was here that Lozen earned the title "The Woman Warrior." In August 1886, after years of desperate battles and escapes, Geronimo sent Lozen and another woman, Dahteste, to meet with representatives of General Nelson Miles in Skeleton Canyon near the Mexican border.

The band turned itself over peacefully to the cavalry, believing that they would be reunited with the wives and children they had left, and eventually permitted to live on the reservations in Arizona. Instead, they were transported by train to Florida. The only photograph that survives of Lozen shows her at the train siding with Geronimo, Naiche, and sixteen other survivors of the band that confounded five thousand soldiers for four years (page 120). Later she was part of a group moved from Florida to the Mount Vernon barracks north of Mobile, Alabama. In the humid and mosquito-infested climate they detested, the Apache suffered and perished of pneumonia and smallpox. Lozen died of tuberculosis in Alabama, where she was buried in an unmarked grave.[15]

## ANNA EARLY GOSEYUN: WHITERIVER, 1994

Anna Goseyun has a way with words. She admits that she has always been outspoken. "From way back, the Apache women always made the decisions. Women were the providers, and men were just the protectors. It is the

*Naiche and Geronimo, front row, third and fourth from left, with their band of Apaches. Lozen is in the top row, at the far right.*

women who have made the center. Now the women go after the jobs. I've always been an activist—it's the activism in me talking out."

Anna Early was born and raised in Cibecue, Arizona, and attended St. John's Indian School in Laveen, five hours away by car. She graduated from Fort Lewis College in Colorado, where she majored in anthropology and art history. She then worked in various positions for the White Mountain Apache Tribe in Whiteriver. From 1976 to 1980, she served her first term as a tribal judge; her most recent service, as a juvenile court judge, ended in 1992. Anna is also an expert and dealer in Apache art and crafts.

Anna married Dan Goseyun and gave birth to four children. She divorced him when Jeanette, the youngest, was just fourteen months old. She has raised her children by herself, and hopes for her daughters that they will also be independent and self-supporting. "I have given them the tools to know how to survive, to think for themselves and keep their thinking caps on. I want them to keep what I've been able to give them of our traditions, to have a good life."

Anna did not have a Sunrise Dance herself, but as a single parent she has given three of these extensive and expensive celebrations for her girls. Anna, raised as a Catholic, came late to the full realization of her traditions. There is no problem for her in reconciling the two sets of beliefs. The Goseyuns' priest, Father Ed Fronzke, attended the girls' dances enthusiastically. Anna spoke easily of the combination of her two spiritual lives.

"I don't think there is a conflict, really. I have been a Catholic all my life. Once I started to learn more about the Apache tradition, I saw that it wasn't so different from Catholicism." She stopped to find just the right words. "Many doctrines taught in the Church are deep, but what I was taught as an Apache was real and practi-

*Anna Early Goseyun*

cal for us as well. Both beliefs make us stronger, I think, but it was traditionalism that made me a whole person."

## BONNIE LAVENDER LEWIS: CIBECUE, 1993

"I am Dishchiidń, from the Bear Clan," says Bonnie Lavender Lewis, a small woman with long black hair just touched with gray. Bonnie is a kindergarten teacher in Cibecue, mother of two teenage sons and stepmother to a toddler daughter.

"More than a hundred years ago, five Navajo women went to fetch water at a river up north, and they were captured by a band of Apache men. They were taken to be servants, but they were treated well and later they married men who came to Fort Apache Reservation. The descendants of these women are called Dishchiidń. My aunt told me the story when I was very little." Bonnie pauses.

"You know, when Apache women were captured by other tribes, they were mistreated, and raped and tattooed." She is anxious to defend Western Apache customs. Bonnie notes that the White Mountain role model remains Alchesay, the gentle scout who led the Fort Apache bands in their peaceful transition to reservation farming life, and not Cochise, Victorio, Mangas Coloradas, or Geronimo.

Bonnie was born in Whiteriver in 1954, and attended the public schools there. She remembers her grade school years as pleasant ones, but the Anglo teachers were strict with the children and smacked them with switches if they spoke Apache. When Bonnie was six, she led a group of her cousins to an abandoned house and played school with them all afternoon. She was the teacher, marching around with a wooden stick, admonishing them in English, "Now you listen!"

As a teenager, Bonnie won mathematics prizes at

Alchesay High School and took "more math classes than anybody." She played the violin and majored in music at Fort Lewis College. Bonnie has been a very active member of the Guenthers' Lutheran congregation at Whiteriver, and taught nursery school at the East Fork Mission School. Her skills in bilingual education have led to several teaching posts and tasks as a professional translator on the reservation. Bonnie's special abilities to combine traditional Apache culture with modern classroom techniques are well known; she has written down Apache legends for children, and believes that she must help the language to survive by teaching the dances and songs.

"Do you know what an 'apple' is?" she asks. "It's an Indian who is red on the outside but white on the inside. Language is the basis of our heritage. It is the main thing. I used to wish that I was white, because white people were rich. I used to imitate them. But when I had my two boys, I taught them only Apache. I told them the stories about Bear and Coyote, and those stories have lessons in them, about discipline and behaving well." She smiles and adds ruefully that since her sons began speaking English in school, their Apache has become rusty.

When Bonnie gives lectures to older children about Apache culture, she says, "You must tell these stories, too. Make sure everybody knows this. We have too many 'apples.'"

*Above us among the mountains the herbs are becoming green.*
*Above us on the tops of the mountains the herbs are becoming yellow.*
*Above us among the mountains, with shoes of yellow I go around the fruits and the herbs that shimmer.*

*Above us among the mountains, the shimmering fruits*
*With shoes and shirts of yellow*
*are bent toward him (the Sun).*
*On the beautiful mountains above, it is daylight.*[16]

# ≈7≈
# Old Age

*He made the black staff of old age for me,*
*He made the road of the sun for me;*
*These holy things he made for me, saying,*
*"With these you will grow old."*
*Now when I have become old,*
*You will remember me by means of them.*[1]

**U**ntil Anglos introduced birth certificates and the idea of keeping track of birthdays and ages, an Apache woman judged herself old not by her years but by her ability to work. Women whom we would consider elderly today continued full and vigorous work, until their strength failed:

> *One day a woman of more than ninety accompanied her daughter out into the hills to gather and roast mescal. Until then she had been unusually active for her age, sometimes walking several*

*miles to gather plants or wood needed at home,*
*but now, when she started cutting the mescal*
*heads, she found herself unable to do the work.*
*Talking of it later, she said, "I tried to cut a*
*mescal head off with the cutting stick, but when I*
*had driven the stick in I didn't have the strength*
*to pull it out again, so I just gave up and rode*
*back to the mescal pit where my daughter was*
*and told her, 'My daughter, from now on you will*
*have to do all the work yourself. I am unable to*
*do it anymore, and I cannot help you. It is as if I*
*was going down to childhood again.'* [2]

A woman was called *bayąąń*, a woman of the "age of reason," from about the ages of forty to sixty. She was referred to as *saáń* after sixty or sixty-five, but as the story illustrates, the *saáń* could still remain a hard worker for many years.

In centuries past, old women acknowledged their diminished role in their families and bands as their abilities waned. Because they were no longer as useful, the old women received as their due the last scraps of the meal, the poorest clothing, the most meager bedding. "This treatment of the old did not lessen family bonds or affection. It was simply accepted that younger people did harder work, and required most of the nourishment and care."[3] The young children they minded when they could no longer go out to work were especially fond of them.

Despite this natural and usually accepted order of life, there were some pathetic moments. Old women sat together and talked wistfully of the time when they could weave beautiful baskets or make perfect buckskin. An elderly grandmother sat inside the wickiup while her family held a *tułkipai* (corn liquor) party outside, to which she had not been invited. "She sat brooding for awhile, and then suddenly burst out crying, at the same time saying so that those outside could hear, 'This is a fine way my own granddaughter is doing to me.' The granddaughter came with a belated cupful soon after, but her grandmother would have none of it."[4]

The older women performed one terrible task: after enemy warriors taken in battle had been interrogated, they were surrounded and killed by the women with axes and spears. Among the Chiricahua, younger women also participated in the carnage.[5]

In times of danger and desperation, when the band suffered from an acute lack of resources or was forced to flee, the aged were sometimes left to die with very little ceremony; this was the way of their world, when their existence threatened the survival of all. They knew this way better even than their children, who were forced to leave them with a little food and water in the wickiup and then to disappear; they too had been compelled to abandon a grandmother or parent this way.

The Apache did not talk about death, and feared the accidental summoning of ghosts. The name of the deceased was never used; references could be made to "she who was your sister," but to speak the name might call back the restless spirit of one who had died. Children whose names had been chosen by the dead person received new ones, although this did not apply to adults. Her spirit stayed close after death, and she longed for her family. In the old times, the camp was immediately moved and was never again revisited. In modern times, when the Apache did not travel about continuously, there were rituals for ridding the home of a ghost.

A woman who died was buried with her possessions, or they were burned with her dwelling. The woman's body was washed and dressed in her best clothing, her hair combed, and her face painted by close female relatives. She was buried in the ground at a remote spot; the grave was covered with rocks so that no animal could

*A photograph from 1880 shows a group of Apache women who had tortured wounded captives.*

desecrate it, and a circle of ashes made around it to keep the spirit from wandering. The mourners left this spot singly and took separate paths, again so that the ghost would not wish to accompany the bereaved family.

Members of the immediate family wept aloud in public during the funeral procession, and often thereafter. On Memorial Day in 1994, women visiting their family graves in the permanent cemetery at Fort Apache wept this way: it is a long, keening cry. Family members cut their hair, wore old clothes, and did not attend social functions, date, or marry for a full year.

The original Apache view of the afterlife has been meshed with later Christian ideas about heaven. The Ndee believed in a life after death that was similar to the life on earth, where the People dwelled together with their families in perpetual peace, joyously repeating the pursuits of the living. The Western Apache spoke of four corners of heaven, all beautiful, from which the deceased woman might choose her permanent rest.

And so the seasons of an Apache women's life had passed. Their substance was duty, nuturance, and unremitting toil—and, also, the joy of recreating and sustaining life. She was Changing Woman, the mother of a people.

# ≈
# Source
# Notes

**Chapter 1**
1. Ronnie Lupe, "At Peace with the Past, in Step with the Future." (*National Geographic*, vol. 157, no. 2, pp. 260–261).

**Chapter 2**
1. Accounts taken from: Keith Basso, *The Cibecue Apache* (New York: Holt, Rinehart: 1970); Basso, *The Gift of Changing Woman,* Smithsonian Institution Bureau of American Ethnology, Bulletin 196 (Washington, D.C.: U.S. Government Printing Office, 1966); Pliny Earle Goddard, *Myths and Tales from the San Carlos Apache* (New York: Anthropological Papers of the American Museum of Natural History, vol. XXIV, part I, 1918); Thomas E. Mails, *Secret Native American Pathways* (Tulsa, Okla.: Council Oak Books, 1988); Morris E. Opler, *An Apache Life-Way* (New York: Cooper Square Publishers, 1965); Opler, *Myths and Tales of the Chiricahua Apache Indians* (Millwood, N.Y.: Kraus Reprint Co., 1976); and Opler, *Myths and Legends of the Lipan Apache Indians,* vol. XXXVI (New York: Memoirs of the American Folk-Lore Society, 1940).

**Chapter 3**

1. From the Closing Songs of the Changing Woman Ceremony, in Morris E. Opler, *An Apache Life-Way*, (New York: Cooper Square Publishers, 1965), p. 130.
2. Opler, p. 127.
3. Anna's words in this chapter are taken both from several author interviews with her and from her article "Carla's Sunrise," which appeared in *Native Peoples*, vol. 4, no. 4, Summer 1991, pp. 8–16. Jeannette's are from interviews with author in June 1994.
4. Opler, p. 127.
5. Keith Basso, *The Gift of Changing Woman*, Smithsonian Institution Bureau of American Ethnology, Bulletin 196 (Washington D.C.: U.S. Government Printing Office, 1966), pp. 142–145.
6. Thomas E. Mails, *Secret Native American Pathways* (Tulsa, Okla.: Council Oak Books, 1988), p. 147.
7. James E. Haley, *Apaches: A History and Cultural Portrait* (Garden City, N.Y.: Doubleday, 1981), p. 135.
8. Mails, p. 154.
9. Basso, p. 158.
10. Grenville Goodwin, *The Social Organization of the Western Apache* (Tucson: University of Arizona Press, 1969), p. 443.
11. Basso, p. 159.
12. Mails, p. 161.
13. Opler, p. 119.
14. Ibid., p. 128.
15. Mails, p. 169.
16. From the Songs of the Girls' Puberty Ceremony, in Harry Hoijer, *Chiricahua and Mescalero Apache Texts* (Chicago: University of Chicago Press, 1938), pp. 49–50.

**Chapter 4**

1. Martha Summerhayes, *Vanished Arizona: Recollecctions of the Army Life of a New England Woman* (Lincoln: University of Nebraska Press, 1979), pp 100–101.

2. Ruth Macdonald Boyer and Narcissus Duffy Gayton, *Apache Mothers and Daughters* (Norman: University of Oklahoma Press, 1992), p. 15.

3. Grenville Goodwin, *The Social Organization of the Western Apache* (Tucson: University of Arizona Press, 1969), p. 454.

4. Goodwin, *Myths and Tales of the White Mountain Apache* (Tucson: University of Arizona Press, 1994), p. 62.

5. Goodwin, *Social Organizations*, p. 499.

6. Morris E. Opler, *An Apache Life-Way* (New York: Cooper Square Publishers, 1965), p. 55–57.

7. Goodwin, *Social Organizations*, p. 458.

8. Boyer and Gayton, p. 210.

9. Ibid., pp. 217–218.

10. Ibid., p. 240.

11. William B. Kessel, "Edgar and Minnie Guenther," in Alan Ferg, ed. *Western Apache Material Culture: The Godwin and Guenther Collections* (Tucson: University of Arizona Press, 1987), p. 12.

## Chapter 5

1. Love Song from Morris E. Opler, *An Apache Life-Way* (New York: Cooper Square Publishers, 1965), p. 125.

2. Grenville Goodwin, *The Social Organization of the Western Apache* (Tucson: University of Arizona Press, 1969), p. 284.

3. D. C. Cole, *The Ciricahua Apache 1846–1876* (Albuquerque: University of New Mexico Press, 1988), p. 18.

4. Opler, p. 125.

5. Goodwin, pp. 302–303.

6. Opler, p. 33.

7. Ibid., p. 144.

8. Goodwin, p. 329.

9. Ruth McDonald Boyer and Narcissus Duffy Gayton, *Apache Mothers and Daughters* (Norman: University of Oklahoma Press, 1992), pp. 80–81.

10. Eve Ball, *Indeh: An Apache Odyssey* (Norman: University of Oklahoma Press, 1988), p. 12.
11. Paula Gunn Allen, *Spider Woman's Granddaughters*, (Boston: Beacon Press, 1989) p. 12.
12. Ball, p. 144.
13. Ibid., pp. 160–164.
14. H. Henrietta Stockel, *Women of the Apache Nation* (Reno: University of Nevada Press, 1991), p. 131.
15. Ibid., p. 143.

*Chapter 6*
1. From the Chiricahua Changing Woman Ceremony, in Morris E. Opler, *An Apache Life-Way* (New York: Cooper Square Publishers, 1965), p. 119.
2. Ruth Macdonald Boyer and Narcissus Duffy Gayton, *Apache Mothers and Daughters* (Norman: University of Oklahoma Press, 1992), p. 17.
3. Eve Ball, *Indeh: An Apache Odyssey* (Norman: University of Oklahoma Press, 1988) p. 102.
4. Grenville Goodwin, "The Social Divisions and Economic Life of the Western Apache," reprinted in Alan Ferg, ed., *Western Apache Material Culture*, The Goodwin and Guenther Collections (Tucson: University of Arizona Press, 1988), p. 46.
5. James L. Haley, *Apaches: A History and Cultural Portrait* (Garden City, N.Y.: Doubleday, 1981), p. 100–101.
6. Exhibit: "Native Peoples of the Southwest," The Heard Museum, Phoenix, Arizona.
7. Carolyn Niethammer, *Daughters of the Earth* (New York: Macmillan, 1977), p. 188.
8. William B. Kessel, "Edgar and Minnie Guenther," in Ferg, p. 147.
9. Haley, p. 147.
10. Eve Ball, *Indeh: An Apache Odyssey*, (Norman: University of Oklahoma Press, 1988), p. 155.

11. Goodwin, *The Social Organization of the Western Apache,* (Tucson: University of Arizona Press, 1969), pp. 342–343.

12. Ball, pp. 204–210.

13. Kimberly Moore Buchanan, *Apache Women Warriors* (El Paso: Texas Western Press, University of Texas at El Paso), pp. 18–26.

14. Ball, pp. 45–46.

15. Accounts taken from: Ball; Dee Brown, *Bury My Heart at Wounded Knee* (New York: Holt, Rinehart, 1970); Boyer and Gayton; Buchanan; Carolyn Niethammer, *Daughters of the Earth* (New York: Macmillan, 1977); David Roberts, "Geronimo," *National Geographic,* vol. 182, no. 4., October 1992, pp. 46–71; and H. Henrietta Stockel, *Women of the Apache Nation* (Reno: University of Nevada Press, 1991).

16. From "The Black Turkey Gobbler Chant," fifty-third Song of the Mescalero ceremony for adolescent girls, transcribed by Pliny E. Goddard, in John Collier, *Rites and Ceremonies of the Indians of the Southwest* (New York: Barnes and Noble, 1993), p. 102.

*Chapter 7:*

1. "Old Age Song," from the Mescalero Sunrise Dance Songs, in Morris E. Opler, *An Apache Life-Way* (New York: Cooper Square Publishers, 1965), p. 128.

2. Grenville Goodwin, *The Social Organization of the Western Apache,* (Tucson: University of Arizona Press, 1969), pp. 512–513.

3. James E. Haley, *Apaches: A History and Cultural Portrait* (Garden City, N.Y.: Doubleday, 1981), p. 171.

4. Goodwin, p. 517.

5. Morris E. Opler, *An Apache Life-Way* (New York: Cooper Square Publishers, 1965), pp. 350–351.

# ≈
# Biblio-
# graphy

Allen, Paula Gunn. *The Sacred Hoop*. Boston: Beacon Press, 1992.

——. *Spider Woman's Granddaughters*. Boston: Beacon Press, 1989.

Ball, Eve. *Indeh: An Apache Odyssey*. Norman: University of Oklahoma Press, 1988.

Basso, Keith. *The Cibecue Apache*. New York: Holt, Rinehart, 1970).

——. *The Gift of Changing Woman*. Smithsonian Institution Bureau of American Ethnology, Bulletin 196. Washington D.C.: U.S. Government Printing Office, 1966.

Boyer, Ruth McDonald, and Narcissus Duffy Gayton. *Apache Mothers and Daughters*. Norman: University of Oklahoma Press, 1992.

Brown, Dee. *Bury My Heart at Wounded Knee*. New York: Holt, Rhinehart, 1970.

Buchanan, Kimberly Moore. *Apache Women Warriors*. El Paso: Texas Western Press, University of Texas at El Paso, 1986.

Cole, D.C. *The Chiricahua Apache 1846–1876.* Albuquerque: University of New Mexico Press, 1988.

Collier, John. *Rites and Ceremonies of the Indians of the Southwest.* New York: Barnes and Noble, 1993.

Ferg, Alan, ed. *Western Apache Material Culture. The Goodwin and Guenther Collections.* Tucson: University of Arizona Press, 1987.

Goddard, Pliny Earle. *Myths and Tales from the San Carlos Apache.* New York: Anthropological Papers of the American Museum of Natural History, vol. XXIV, part I, 1918.

Goodwin, Grenville. *Myths and Tales of the White Mountain Apache.* Tucson: University of Arizona Press, 1994.

——. *The Social Organization of the Western Apache.* Tucson: University of Arizona Press, 1969.

Goseyun, Anna. "Carla's Sunrise." *Native Peoples,* vol. 4, no. 4, Summer 1991, pp. 8–16.

Haley, James E. *Apaches: A History and Culture Portrait.* Garden City, N.Y.: Doubleday, 1981.

Hoijer, Harry. *Chiracahua and Mescalero Apache Texts.* Chicago: University of Chicago Press, 1938.

Lupe, Ronnie. "At Peace with the Past, in Step with the Future." *National Geographic,* vol. 157, no. 2, pp. 260–261.

Mails, Thomas E. *Secret Native American Pathways.* Tulsa, Okla.: Council Oak Books, 1988.

"Native Peoples of the Southwest." Permanent exhibit, The Heard Museum, Phoenix, Ariz.

Niethammer, Carolyn. *Daughters of the Earth.* New York: Macmillan, 1977.

Opler, Morris E. *An Apache Life-Way.* New York: Cooper Square Publishers, 1965.

——. *Myths and Legends of the Lipan Apache Indians.* New York: Memoirs of the American Folk-Lore Society, vol. XXXVI, 1940.

——. *Myths and Tales of the Chiricahua Apache Indians*. Millwood, N.Y.: Kraus Reprint Co., 1976.

Roberts, David. "Geronimo." *National Geographic,* vol. 182, no. 4, October 1992, pp. 46–71.

Stockel, H. Henrietta. *Women of the Apache Nation.* Reno: University of Nevada Press, 1991.

Summerhayes, Martha. *Vanished Arizona: Recollections of the Army Life of a New England Woman.* Lincoln: University of Nebraska Press, 1979.

### Suggested Internet Resources
Brief tribal histories and biographies are available here: http://www.cs.umu.se/~dphln/wildwest/indians.html

"Frontier Internet" site features resources for teachers and students of American Indian culture (Example: a Coyote story): http://www.durango.net/southwest.html

# Index